Rumors

A FARCE

RUMORS

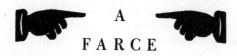

A

FARCE

BY

Neil Simon

RANDOM HOUSE NEW YORK

Library of Congress Cataloging-in-Publication Data-Reg.
Simon, Neil.
Rumors: a farce/by Neil Simon.
p. cm.
ISBN 0-394-58799-5
I. Title.
PS3537.I663R8   1991
812'.54—dc20   90-52998

FOR GENE SAKS

Rumors by Neil Simon was produced by The Old Globe Theatre in San Diego, California. It opened on September 22, 1988, with the following cast:

CHRIS GORMAN	Christine Baranski
KEN GORMAN	Mark Nelson
CLAIRE GANZ	Jessica Walter
LENNY GANZ	Ron Leibman
ERNIE CUSACK	Andre Gregory
COOKIE CUSACK	Joyce Van Patten
GLENN COOPER	Ken Howard
CASSIE COOPER	Lisa Banes
OFFICER WELCH	Charles Brown
OFFICER PUDNEY	Cynthia Darlow

Rumors was directed by Gene Saks. The set was designed by Tony Straiges, the lighting was designed by Tharon Musser, and the costumes were designed by Joseph G. Aulisi. Douglas Pagliotti was the production stage manager.

Rumors by Neil Simon was subsequently produced by Emanuel Azenberg at the Broadhurst Theatre in New York City. It opened on November 17, 1988, with the following cast:

CHRIS GORMAN	Christine Baranski
KEN GORMAN	Mark Nelson
CLAIRE GANZ	Jessica Walter
LENNY GANZ	Ron Leibman
ERNIE CUSACK	Andre Gregory

COOKIE CUSACK	Joyce Van Patten
GLENN COOPER	Ken Howard
CASSIE COOPER	Lisa Banes
OFFICER WELCH	Charles Brown
OFFICER PUDNEY	Cynthia Darlow

Rumors was directed by Gene Saks. The set was designed by Tony Straiges, the lighting was designed by Tharon Musser, the costumes were designed Joseph G. Aulisi, and the sound was designed by Tom Morse. Peter Lawrence was the production stage manager.

 *Act One*

We are in a large, tastefully renovated, Victorian house in Sneden's Landing, New York, about forty minutes from the city. Despite its age and gingerbread exterior, the interior is white, modern, monochromatic, and sparkling clean. A nice combination.

An entrance doorway at upstage right leads to an open vestibule. To the right of the door is a powder room. One step down is the large and comfortable living room.

There are two furniture groupings in the living room. At stage right are a love seat and two chairs. Upstage of the love seat and near the powder room door is a table and a telephone with a long cord. At center stage are a large sofa and coffee table. Two chairs at stage left are part of a grouping with the sofa. On the stage left wall is a mirror in an ornate frame. Against the upstage wall are a well-stocked bar and a stereo system enclosed in a gorgeous cabinet. Between these two pieces is a closed door leading to the cellar.

From the living room, a curved staircase leads to a landing and two doors, each leading to a bedroom. On the landing is a railed banister. At the stage left end of the second-floor landing is an archway leading to a hallway and more bedrooms. Downstage of this archway is an extension of the balcony which can be used as a playing area.

Through the living room, at left, double doors lead into a dining room and then to the kitchen. A huge window above the front door looks out onto a wooded backyard. A large window in the stage right wall overlooks a yard and the driveway beyond. Headlights of approaching cars may be seen through this window.

It is about eight-thirty P.M. on a pleasant evening in May.

CHRIS GORMAN, *an attractive woman in her mid-thirties, paces anxiously back and forth, looking at her watch and biting her nails. She is elegantly dressed in a designer evening gown. She looks at the phone, then at her watch again. She seems to make a decision and goes for the cigarette box on the coffee table. She takes a cigarette from the box, then puts it back.*

CHRIS Oh, my God!

> *(Suddenly, on the landing,* CHARLEY*'s bedroom door opens and* KEN GORMAN, *about forty, dressed smartly in a tuxedo but looking flushed and excited, comes out to the railing. Both he and* CHRIS *speak rapidly)*

KEN Did he call yet?

CHRIS Wouldn't I have yelled up?

KEN Call him again.

CHRIS I called him twice. They're looking for him . . . How is he?

KEN I'm not sure. He's bleeding like crazy.

CHRIS Oh, my God!

KEN It's all over the room. I don't know why people decorate in white . . . If he doesn't call in two minutes, call the hospital.

CHRIS I'm going to have to have a cigarette, Ken.

KEN After eighteen months, the hell you are. Hold on to yourself, will you?

> *(He rushes back in and closes the door behind him. She goes back to pacing)*

CHRIS I can't believe this is happening. *(She goes for the cigarette box again. The phone rings)* Oh, God! *(She calls out)* Ken, the phone is ringing. *(But he's gone. She goes to the phone and picks it up)* Hello? Dr. Dudley? . . . Oh, Dr. Dudley, I'm so glad it's you. Your service said you were at the theater.

(CHARLEY's bedroom door opens. KEN looks out)

KEN Is that the doctor?

CHRIS *(Into the phone)* I never would have bothered you, but this is an emergency.

KEN Is that the doctor?

CHRIS *(Into the phone)* I'm Chris Gorman. My husband, Ken, and I are good friends of Charley Brock's.

KEN Is that the doctor?

CHRIS *(She turns, holds the phone, and yells at KEN)* It's the doctor! It's the doctor!

KEN *(Angrily)* Why didn't you say so?

(He goes back in and closes the door)

CHRIS *(Into the phone)* Dr. Dudley, I'm afraid there's been an accident . . . I would have called my own doctor, but my husband is a lawyer and under the circumstances, he thought it better to have Charley's own physician . . . Well, we just arrived here at Charley's house about ten minutes ago, and as we were getting out of our car, we suddenly heard this enormous—

5

(KEN *suddenly comes out of the bedroom*)

KEN   Don't say anything!

CHRIS *(To* KEN*)*   What?

KEN   Don't tell him what happened!

CHRIS   Don't tell him?

KEN   Just do what I say.

CHRIS   What about Charley?

KEN   He's all right. It's just a powder burn. Don't tell him about the gunshot.

CHRIS   But they got the doctor out of the theater.

KEN   Tell him he tripped down the stairs and banged his head. He's all right.

CHRIS   But what about the blood?

KEN   The bullet went through his earlobe. It's nothing. I don't want him to know.

CHRIS   But I already said we were getting out of the car and we suddenly heard an enormous—what? What did we hear?

KEN *(Coming downstairs)*   We heard . . .

CHRIS *(Into the phone)*   Just a minute, Doctor.

KEN *(He thinks as he's coming downstairs)* We heard
. . . we heard . . . we heard . . . an enormous—*thud!*

CHRIS Thud?

KEN When he tripped down the stairs.

CHRIS Good. Good. That's good. *(Into the phone)* Dr.
Dudley? I'm sorry. I was just talking to my husband.
Well, we heard this enormous *thud!* It seemed Charley
tripped going up the stairs.

KEN *Down!* Down the stairs.

CHRIS *Down* the stairs. But he's all right.

KEN He's sitting up in bed. He'll call him in the morning.

CHRIS He's sitting up in bed. He'll call him in the morning.

KEN *You!*

CHRIS *You!* He'll call *you* in the morning.

KEN You're very sorry you disturbed him.

CHRIS I'm very sorry I disturbed you.

KEN But he's really fine.

CHRIS But he's really fine.

KEN Thank you and good-bye.

CHRIS *(To* KEN*)*   Where are you going?

KEN   *Him! Him!* Thank him and say good-bye.

CHRIS   Oh. *(Into phone)* Thank you and good-bye, Doctor . . . What? . . . Just a minute. *(To* KEN *as he goes upstairs)* Any dizziness?

KEN   No. No dizziness.

CHRIS *(Into phone)*   No. Dizziness . . .What? *(To* KEN*)* Can he move his limbs?

KEN *(Irritated)*   Yes! He can move everything. Get off the phone.

CHRIS *(Yells at* KEN*)*   They got him out of *Phantom of the Opera.* *(Into phone)* Yes, he can move everything . . . What? *(To* KEN*)* Any slurring of the speech?

KEN   NO! NO SLURRING OF THE SPEECH.

CHRIS *(To* KEN, *without covering phone)*   Don't yell at me. He'll hear it. *(Into phone)* No. No slurring of the speech.

KEN   I've got to get back to Charley.

   *(*KEN *starts to go back to* CHARLEY*'s room)*

CHRIS *(Into the phone)*   Any what? *(To* KEN*)* Any ringing of the ears?

KEN   I can't believe this . . . No. Tell him no.

CHRIS *(Into the phone)*   Yes. A little ringing in the ears.

KEN   I told you to say no.

CHRIS   It sounds more believable to have ringing.

KEN   Jesus!

CHRIS *(Into the phone)*   . . . Who? His wife? Myra? . . . Yes. Myra's here.

KEN *(Rushing downstairs)*   She's *not* here. Don't tell him she's here. He'll want to speak to her.

CHRIS *(Into the phone)*   Dr. Dudley? My mistake. She's not here. I thought she was but she wasn't.

KEN   She just stepped out. She'll be back in a minute.

CHRIS *(Into the phone)*   She just stepped back. She'll be out in a minute. Yes. I'll tell her to call. *(KEN goes back upstairs)* . . . Okay, thank you, Dr. Diddley . . . Dudley. Enjoy the show. Ken and I saw it, we loved it . . . Especially the second act. Who's playing the Phantom tonight?

KEN   Are you going to review the whole goddamn show?

(KEN *goes back into* CHARLEY'*s room)*

CHRIS   Oh, Charley's calling me. *(Calling out)* Just a minute, Charley. *(Into the phone)* He sounds a lot better. I have to go. Yes, Doctor, I will. Thank you so much, Dr. Pudley . . . Dudley! *(She bangs up, furious at*

KEN) Don't you *ever* do that to me again. He must suspect something. I didn't get his name right once.

KEN *(Coming out of the bedroom)*   If anyone calls again, don't answer it.

(He starts to go into the bedroom)

CHRIS   Then why did you tell me to answer that one?

KEN   Because I thought the bullet went through his head, not his earlobe. Fix me a double vodka, I left Charley standing in the shower.

CHRIS   If he drowns, you're making that call. *(KEN goes into the bedroom)* I don't know why we're always the first ones here. *(She fixes the vodka)* Never came late once in our lives. Someone else could have dealt with all this. *(She goes to the cigarette box once more. The doorbell rings. She jumps)* Oh, SHIT! Shit shit shit shit!

(The upstairs door opens and KEN comes out)

KEN   Who's that? Who is that?

CHRIS   Am I near the door? Do you see people in here? You think I'm on roller skates?

KEN   Let me think a minute.

CHRIS   Take your time because I don't answer doors. I only speak to Dr. Dudley.

KEN   All right. It's got to be Lenny or Ernie, one of the others. We've got to open the door.

CHRIS You've got arms, reach down.

KEN I've got to dry Charley off and bandage his ear. Don't tell them what happened. I need a few minutes to figure this out. Can't you stall them?

CHRIS His best friends are coming to his tenth anniversary, his wife isn't here, he shoots himself in the earlobe, and I'm supposed to make small talk when they come in?

KEN Attempted suicide is a criminal offense, not to mention a pretty ugly scandal. Charlie's deputy mayor of New York. He's my client and my best friend. I've got to protect him, don't I? Just play the hostess for a few minutes until I figure out how to handle this.

(*The doorbell rings again*)

CHRIS Play the hostess? There's no food out, there's no ice in the bucket. Where's the help? Where's the cheese dip? Where's Myra? What am I supposed to do till you get back, play charades? I'm lucky I can still speak English.

KEN You're a lawyer yourself, can't you figure out something to say?

CHRIS Contracts! I draw up legal publishing contracts. If someone walks in the door and wants to make a deal, I CAN HANDLE THAT!!

KEN Take it easy. Calm down. I'll be right back.

(*The doorbell rings again*)

CHRIS   Put some slippers on Charlie and tell *him* to answer it.

KEN *(Yelling)*   Would you relax? Drink my vodka.

CHRIS   Why is a vodka better than two puffs of a cigarette?

KEN   Because they know you quit and if they see smoke in here, they'll know something is wrong.

CHRIS   You mean falling at their feet is going to look better? *(The doorbell rings impatiently.* KEN *runs into the bedroom and closes the door.* CHRIS *crosses to the front door. She opens it.* CLAIRE *rushes into the living room. She's an attractive woman in an evening gown. She is holding a handkerchief to the side of her mouth, a purse in her other hand)* Claire, darling, you look beautiful. Where's Lenny?

CLAIRE *(Coming in)*   In the car. We had an accident. Brand-new BMW, two days old, the side door is smashed in. Don't tell Charley and Myra, I don't want to ruin tonight for them.

(She goes to the mirror and looks at her face)

CHRIS   Oh, my God! Are you hurt?

CLAIRE   My lip is swelling up. *(She looks in the wall mirror)* Oh, Jesus, I look like a trumpet player.

CHRIS   Where's Lenny?

CLAIRE He's coming. He's walking slowly, he's got whiplash. His seat belt went right around his neck and pulled him straight up. I left him dangling.

CHRIS Oh, sweetheart, I'm sorry. Is there anything I can do?

CLAIRE Just don't tell Myra. This party means so much to her.

> (LENNY *comes in through the front door. He's wearing a tuxedo and is holding the back of his neck with one hand, and is carrying a gift box from Steuben in his other arm*)

LENNY *(He's in pain, but he smiles. His neck is stiff)* Hi, Charley! Hi, Myra! We're here, kids.

CHRIS They're upstairs, Lenny.

LENNY *(To CHRIS)* Did she tell you what happened? Some stupid bastard shoots out of his garage like a Polaris rocket. I've got four doors on one side of the car now.

CHRIS How does your neck feel?

LENNY Stretched out, over to one side. I look like a Modigliani painting.

> *(He goes over to the phone and picks it up)*

CHRIS Do you want a drink?

LENNY I don't think I could swallow past my shoulders.

CLAIRE   Of all nights to happen.

LENNY   Here's their gift. Steuben glass. *(He shakes the box. Broken glass rattles)* If someone brings them a bottle of glue, they'll have a nice gift.

(He starts to dial, carefully)

CLAIRE *(She looks at her mouth in a hand mirror)*   I could have lost the tip of my tongue. I'd be speaking Gaelic the rest of my life.

LENNY *(Waiting on the phone)*   A brand-new, spotless car, never touched by human hands. Buffed and polished by German women in Munich and now it looks like a war memorial. *(Into the phone)* Hello? This is Leonard Ganz. Is Dr. Dudley there, please?

CHRIS   Dr. Dudley?

LENNY *(Into the phone)*   Yes, it is. I have a whiplash injury . . . I see . . . Do you know what theater he's in?

CHRIS   Oh, God, I need a cigarette so badly.

LENNY   Could you? It's important. I'm at—*(He looks at the phone)* 914-473-2261 . . . Thank you very much.

(He hangs up)

CLAIRE   I've got to settle my stomach. Is there anything to eat? Some canapés or something?

CHRIS   Gee, I don't see anything.

CLAIRE No canapés? Where's the cook, Mai Li? She makes great canapés.

CHRIS Mai Li? I didn't see her. I think she's off this week.

CLAIRE The week of their anniversary party?

CHRIS I think she had to go back to Japan. Her mother was sick.

CLAIRE Mai Li is Chinese.

CHRIS I know. Her mother was visiting Japan.

LENNY *(Still bracing his neck)* I can only look up. I hope tall people are coming to this party . . . Where's Ken?

CHRIS Ken? He went to the bathroom.

LENNY And where's Charley and Myra?

CHRIS They're still getting dressed.

LENNY They're not ready. We had a *car* accident and we're on time.

CLAIRE *(She looks in the hand mirror again)* My lip is getting gigantic. I don't think I have enough lipstick to cover it.

LENNY No nuts or pretzels? I didn't even have lunch today. Three goddamn audits with the IRS on an empty stomach. *(He gets up)* Claire, get me a Diet Coke, please, and something to munch on.

(He starts for the stairs)

CHRIS   Where are you going?

LENNY   To the john. I haven't had a chance to do that either.

CHRIS   There's a guest powder room down here.

LENNY   Isn't Ken using that?

CHRIS   No, he's using the one in the guest bedroom upstairs.

LENNY *(Pointing to the powder room)*   Why didn't he use this one?

CHRIS   I don't know. He said he had to go badly and he ran upstairs.

LENNY   If he had to go so bad, the one downstairs is closer.

CHRIS   You know how it is when you have to go badly. You don't want to stop running.

LENNY   But this is a shorter run.

CLAIRE   Lenny, it's not an Olympic event. Why don't you just go?

LENNY   That's why they build guest bathrooms. *(He starts for the powder room)* If Dr. Dudley calls, I'll be right out.

   (He goes into the powder room and closes the door)

CHRIS Claire, we have to talk.

(CLAIRE *goes to sit near* CHRIS)

CLAIRE What is it?

CHRIS I'm coming apart at the seams.

CLAIRE Your dress?

CHRIS No, my nerves. I think I'm going to crack.

CLAIRE I can see. *(Taking* CHRIS*'s hand)* Your hands are like ice. Something is going on here, isn't it?

CHRIS Oh, God, you're so smart. You're so quick to see things.

CLAIRE You're scaring me, Chris. Tell me what's happening.

CHRIS Well, all right. Ken and I arrived here about ten minutes ago, when suddenly we heard this enormous . . .

(CHARLEY*'s bedroom door opens.* KEN *steps out)*

KEN Hey, Claire! You look lovely.

CHRIS Yes! I was just telling her that. She looks *enormously* well, doesn't she? *(To* CLAIRE*)* Isn't that the dress you wore for Cerebral Palsy?

CLAIRE No. I got this for Sickle Cell. Hi, Ken.

KEN Where's Lenny?

CLAIRE He's in the john. Where's Charley and Myra?

CHRIS *(To* KEN*)* Still getting dressed?

KEN Yes. Still getting dressed . . . How's the new BMW? Is Len happy with it?

CLAIRE Delirious.

KEN Did he get the new features he asked for?

CLAIRE More than he asked for.

KEN Great.

CLAIRE Are you through in the bathroom, Ken? I have to go myself. *(She starts for the stairs)*

KEN I think Myra's in there.

CLAIRE Then I'll use Mai Li's bathroom. Call me if she gets back from Japan.

(She goes into the kitchen)

KEN *(Waving his arms at* CHRIS*)* Up here! Quick! *(*CHRIS *rushes up the stairs)* Hurry up! *(Breathlessly, she gets there)* What did you tell her?

CHRIS I can't remember.

KEN You can't remember?

CHRIS   I couldn't follow it, I was talking so fast. Why can't we tell them the truth? They're going to find out anyway.

KEN   I don't *know* the truth yet. Charley is still mumbling. Now go inside. He wants to see you.

CHRIS   See *me?* Why does he want to see me?

KEN   He's crying like a baby. I can't stop him. He needs a woman.

CHRIS   . . . To do what?

KEN   To cry on. I can reason with him but I can't comfort him. Let him cry on your shoulder for two minutes, for chrisakes.

CHRIS   *(Starting into* CHARLEY's *room)*   Is he still bleeding? I paid twelve hundred dollars for this dress.

(She goes in and closes the door just as LENNY *comes out of the powder room)*

KEN   Oh, hi, Len!

LENNY   *(He looks up and winces)*   Oh, Jesus. *(He grabs his neck)* Hi, Ken. Did you hear about the BMW?

KEN   Yeah. Congratulations. Excuse me.

(He turns to go)

LENNY   Where are you going?

KEN   To the john.

LENNY   Didn't you just go?

KEN   . . . Yes. But not enough. Be right with you.

(He goes into the guest room, just as CLAIRE *comes out of the kitchen with a bag of pretzels, unopened)*

CLAIRE   This is very weird.

LENNY   Give me the pretzels.

(He grabs the bag. She pours two Cokes)

CLAIRE   There's plenty of food in the kitchen, but nothing's cooked.

LENNY   Why didn't you open this first?

(He struggles with the bag)

CLAIRE   There's a duck, roast ham, smoked turkey, all defrosting on the table. There's pasta sitting in a pot with no water. (LENNY *can't open the bag. He bites into it)* Everything's ready to go, but no one's there to start it. Doesn't that seem strange to you?

LENNY   Not as strange as him peeing twice in a row . . . Have you got something sharp, a nail file or something?

CLAIRE   Chris started to tell me something and then she clammed up.

LENNY   The door on my BMW opened like tissue paper but this thing is like steel.

CLAIRE   Her hands were as cold as ice. She couldn't look me straight in the eye.

LENNY   This would be a safe place to keep your jewelry!! *(He tries one last time to open it, then throws it away)* Goddamnit!!

CLAIRE   And why are they taking so long to get dressed? What is that about, heh?

LENNY   What are you so damn suspicious for? Give the people a chance to come down.

CLAIRE   Oh, you don't notice anything is wrong?

LENNY   Yes, I noticed. I noticed the towels in the bathroom were piled up on the sink and not on the rack. I noticed there's only a sheet and a half left on the toilet paper. I think it's sloppy, but not a scandal.

CLAIRE   Really? Well, I'm not so sure I'd rule out a scandal.

(She walks away from him)

LENNY   You think I don't know what you're talking about? I hear what's going on. I hear gossip, I hear rumors, and I won't listen to that crap, you understand. He is my friend, she is the wife of my friend.

CLAIRE   Fine! Okay, then forget it.

LENNY   I don't listen to filth and garbage about my friends.

CLAIRE   I said forget it.

LENNY   *(He looks at her)*. . . All right. Come here.

> *(He walks to the extreme downstage right corner of the living room)*

CLAIRE   What's wrong with here?

LENNY   They could hear us there. Here is better. Will you come here! *(She goes to him. He looks around, then at her)* It's not good.

CLAIRE   What's not good?

LENNY   What I heard.

CLAIRE   What did you hear?

LENNY   Will you lower your voice?

CLAIRE   Why? We haven't said anything yet.

LENNY   All right. There's talk going around about Myra and—This hurts me. Stand on my other side. I can't turn. *(She turns with her back to him. He moves to her other side)* There's talk going around about Myra and Charley. Only no one will tell it to my face because they know I won't listen.

CLAIRE   I'll listen. Tell it to my face.

LENNY   Why would you want to hear things about our best friends? He's my best client. He trusts me. Not just about investments and taxes, but personal things.

CLAIRE   I don't do his taxes, what's the rumors?

LENNY   Jesus, you won't be satisfied till you hear, will you?

CLAIRE   I won't even *sleep* with you until I hear. What's the rumors?

LENNY   . . . All right. Your friend Myra upstairs is having herself a little thing, okay?

CLAIRE   What kind of thing?

LENNY   Do I have to spell it out? A thing. A guy. A man. A fella. A kid. An affair. She's doing something with someone on the sly somewhere and it's not with Charley. Okay?

CLAIRE   You don't know that. You only heard it. You haven't seen it.

LENNY   Of course I haven't seen it. You think they invite me to come along? What's wrong with you?

CLAIRE   You are so naïve, it's incredible. Get real, Lenny. Myra's not having anything with anybody. Your friend, Charley, however, is running up a hell of a motel bill.

LENNY   Charley? My friend Charley? No way. Not a chance. He wouldn't even look at another woman.

CLAIRE   He may not be looking at her, but he's screwing her.

LENNY   Will you lower your voice! . . . Where did you hear this?

CLAIRE   Someone at the tennis club told me.

LENNY   *Our* tennis club?

CLAIRE   What is it, a sacred temple? People gossip there.

LENNY   Christ! Bunch of hypocrites. Sit around in their brand-new Nikes and Reeboks destroying people's lives . . . Who told you this?

CLAIRE   I'm not going to tell you because you don't like this person anyway.

LENNY   What's the difference if I like them or not? Who told you?

CLAIRE   Carole Newman.

LENNY   CAROLE NEWMAN?? I knew it, I knew it. I *hate* that goddamn woman. She's got a mouth big enough to swallow a can of tennis balls.

(*The guest room door opens and* KEN *steps out onto the landing*)

KEN (*Affably*)   How you two doing?

LENNY   Hey! Just fine, Ken.

KEN   Had anything to eat yet?

LENNY   Just a plastic bag.

KEN   Great! Be right back.

(KEN *goes into* CHARLEY's *bedroom and closes the door*)

LENNY   Wasn't it Carole Newman who spread the other rumor?

CLAIRE   What other rumor?

LENNY   The rumor that you and I were breaking up.

CLAIRE   No. It wasn't Carole Newman.

LENNY   It wasn't? Then who was it?

CLAIRE   It was me.

LENNY   *You* started the rumor?

CLAIRE   Me, you, the both of us. When we were thinking about separating, didn't we go around telling everyone?

LENNY   We told friends. That bitch told strangers.

CLAIRE   Hey! Hey! Do *not* call Carole Newman a bitch to my face. Besides, Carole Newman didn't start the rumor about Charley. Someone else at the club told her.

(*She walks to the bar*)

LENNY   Who was the one who told her?

CLAIRE   Harold Green.

LENNY   Harold Green? Who the hell is Harold Green?

CLAIRE   He's a new member. He was just voted in last week.

LENNY   I never voted for him.

CLAIRE   Yes, you did. By proxy. We were in Bermuda.

LENNY   I don't believe it. A goddamn proxy new member spreads rumors about my best friend? Who does he play tennis with?

CLAIRE   He doesn't play tennis. He's a social member. He just eats lunches there.

LENNY   . . . This son of a bitch is a non-playing proxy social new member who just eats lunches and spreads rumors? What does he do for a living?

CLAIRE   He sells BMWs.

(CHARLEY's *bedroom door opens and* KEN *steps out*)

KEN   Did anyone else get here yet?

CLAIRE   Not to speak of, no.

LENNY   Is anything wrong?

KEN *(Coming downstairs)*   Why? Does anything seem wrong to you?

LENNY   You mean aside from the fact there's no food, no guests, no host, no hostess, and that you and Chris only appear one at a time and never together? Yes, I'd say something was wrong.

KEN   Okay. *(He looks at the floor, thinking)* Okay, sit down, Len, Claire. *(LENNY and CLAIRE sit. KEN sits in the chair opposite them)* All right, I can't keep this quiet anymore . . . We've got a big problem on our hands.

LENNY *(To CLAIRE)*   Aha! What did I just say, Claire?

CLAIRE   You just said "Aha!" *(To KEN)* What is it, Ken? Tell us.

KEN   Charley . . . Charley, er . . . Charley's been shot.

CLAIRE   *WHAT???*

LENNY   *SHOT???*

CLAIRE   Oh, my God!

LENNY   Jesus Christ!

CLAIRE   Don't tell me this!

LENNY   I can't catch my breath.

CLAIRE   Please don't let it be true.

LENNY *(He wails)*   *Charley, Charley, no! No, Charley, no!!!*

KEN   Take it easy, he's not dead. He's all right.

CLAIRE   He's not dead?

LENNY   He's all right?

KEN   He's alive. He's okay.

LENNY   Thank God, he's alive!

CLAIRE   Where was he shot?

KEN   In the head.

CLAIRE   In the *head?* The *head?* Oh, my God, he was shot in the *head!!!*

KEN   It's all right. It's not bad. It's a superficial wound.

LENNY   Where did the bullet go?

KEN   Through his left earlobe.

CLAIRE   The earlobe? That's not too bad. I have holes in my earlobes, it doesn't hurt.

LENNY   I saw this coming, I swear. The truth, Ken, did *she* do it?

KEN   Who?

LENNY   Myra, for chrissakes. Who else would it be?

KEN   Why would Myra shoot Charley?

CLAIRE   You don't know what's going on?

LENNY   You haven't heard?

KEN No. What's going on?

CLAIRE Charley's been having a hot affair with someone.

LENNY It's not hot. You don't know if it's hot. Nobody said it was hot. *(To KEN)* It's an affair. A plain affair.

KEN *(To LENNY)* Who told you this?

LENNY Nobody told me *that*. What I heard was that *Myra* was having a thing.

KEN A thing with who?

LENNY A man. A guy. A fellow. A kid. Who knows?

CLAIRE Someone else told me it was *Charley* who was having the affair.

KEN What someone else?

LENNY Some bitch at the club named Carole Newman.

CLAIRE She is *not* a bitch. And she only told me what Harold Green told her.

KEN Who's Harold Green?

LENNY *(Quickly)* Some goddamn proxy new social member who doesn't even play tennis. Comes to the club to eat lunches and spread rumors.

CLAIRE Well, it seems to me Charley's the one who's having the affair if Myra was hysterical enough to shoot him.

KEN Listen to me, will you, please? Myra didn't shoot him. *Charley* fired the gun. He tried to kill himself. It was attempted suicide.

CLAIRE *SUICIDE???*

LENNY Jesus Christ!

CLAIRE Oh, my God!

LENNY Don't tell me that.

CLAIRE I don't believe it.

LENNY *(He wails)* No, Charley, no! Charley, Charley, no!

KEN Will you stop it! It's enough grieving. He's all right.

CLAIRE Oh, Charley.

LENNY It's all because of that no-good fucking Harold Green. That guy's out of the club. I can get the votes.

KEN Can we stick to the main topic here? Nobody knows if anybody had an affair. I don't *know* why Charley shot himself.

LENNY *(To* KEN*)* So how is Myra taking this? My God, she must be a wreck.

CLAIRE *(Rising)* I should go up to her. Let me go up to her.

KEN *(Stopping* CLAIRE*)*   Don't go up to her. There's no point in going up to her. She's not here. She's gone.

CLAIRE   She's gone? Charley shoots himself in the head and Myra leaves the house?

LENNY   She walks out on him *now? Now* when he's lying up there with a bullet in his ear?

KEN   It's not in his ear. It went *through* his ear. WILL YOU LISTEN TO ME? PLEASE!!! . . . Maybe she wasn't even here when it happened. Chris and I were driving up when we heard the shot. The front door was locked. I ran around the back and broke in the kitchen window.

CLAIRE   I saw that. I thought maybe Mai Li did it and maybe Myra fired her. But I didn't know then that Mai Li's mother was sick in Japan.

LENNY *(To* CLAIRE*)*   Don't talk for a while. Let me and Ken talk. You just listen. *(To* KEN*)* So you broke in and rushed upstairs. Was he on the floor?

KEN   No. He was sitting in bed. The television was on. One of those Evangelist shows. A bottle of Valium was on the night table. He was half-conscious. I figured maybe he took a couple of pills to make himself drowsy, put the gun to his head, started to fall asleep, and shot himself through the ear.

CLAIRE   Is that blood on your shirt, Ken?

KEN *(Looking down at his shirt)*   Where?

CLAIRE   Below the second stud.

KEN   Oh, shit, I didn't see that. That won't come out, will it?

LENNY   That's what you're worried about? A stain on your dress shirt?

KEN   I don't give a damn about my shirt. I'm trying to prevent Charley from getting a suicide rap. When the others walk in here, I don't want to explain to them how I got blood on my good silk shirt.

CLAIRE   You could borrow one of Charley's.

KEN   He's two sizes too big for me.

CLAIRE   I don't think they'd notice your cuffs if Charley has a big bandage on his ear and Myra's not even at the party.

LENNY   Let the man finish the story, will you, please? (*To* KEN) Did he tell you anything? Did he say why he did it?

KEN   Not a word. He was barely conscious.

LENNY   Did he leave a note or anything?

KEN   He had a piece of paper in his hand. I tried to take it from him, but he tore it up and threw it into the john. He flushed before I could get to it.

CLAIRE   Did you call the police?

KEN   No. Just his doctor. We told him he fell down the stairs. As long as he wasn't hurt, I didn't want to make this thing public.

LENNY   We've *got* to call the police. This man is the deputy mayor of New York. We're talking front page on *The New York Times*. Pictures of Charley with his suit jacket over his head.

KEN   Exactly. That's what I'm trying to avoid till we find out what happened.

LENNY   If we keep this quiet, we're all accessories. I deal with the IRS boys. I'd be the first one they'd go after.

KEN   Why would they go after you?

LENNY   With attempted suicides, they open up everything. They'd want to see his books, his portfolio, his entire financial picture. They'd want to know how a deputy mayor could afford a big house like this.

KEN   That's no secret. Myra's a wealthy woman. She bought the house.

CLAIRE   She did? I didn't know that.

LENNY   *(To KEN)*   You hear that? Now tomorrow it'll be all over the tennis club.

KEN   I'm not bringing in the police until I have to. I don't know what *you're* nervous about. Unless you have something to hide you don't want the IRS to know.

LENNY   Are you accusing me of hiding something? I'm the one who wants to bring in the police. Maybe *you're* the one who has something to hide. You make out his contracts. You made out his will.

KEN   Are you accusing me and Charley of conspiracy to defraud the city?

(We see headlights flash on the window)

CLAIRE   I hear a car pulling up.

LENNY *(To* KEN, *starting for the phone)*   If you're not calling the police, I am.

KEN   Oh no you're not.

LENNY   You're telling me what I'm not going to do?

CLAIRE *(At the window)*   It's pulling up the driveway.

LENNY   Suppose the neighbors heard the gunshot and have already called the police.

KEN   I'll deal with that problem when it arises.

LENNY   Maybe the car is the police. Then the problem has arosen.

CLAIRE *(Looking out the window)*   It's a Volvo station wagon.

LENNY   A Volvo??!

KEN   Now I suppose you're worried it's the Swedish police.

CLAIRE It's Ernie and Cookie.

LENNY Ernie and Cookie?

KEN *(To* CLAIRE*)* Why didn't you tell us?

CLAIRE Why didn't you listen?

> *(*LENNY *and* KEN *join* CLAIRE *at the window.* CHAR-LEY*'s bedroom door opens and* CHRIS *steps out)*

CHRIS Ken, Myra and I are having trouble with her zipper.

KEN No, you're not.

CHRIS I'm not?

KEN They know about it.

CHRIS About Myra's zipper?

LENNY We know that Myra's not here. Ken told us.

CHRIS Oh.

CLAIRE *(At the window)* They're stopping to look at our BMW.

CHRIS Did you tell them about Charley cutting his ear shaving?

KEN They know *everything*. The gunshot, the earlobe, the flushed note down the toilet, everything.

CHRIS *(Angrily to* KEN, *as she comes downstairs)   Why didn't you tell me you told them??* . . . They must think I'm an idiot.

LENNY   How is Charley?

CHRIS   He fell asleep. He's hugging the pillow with his thumb in his mouth.

CLAIRE   They're coming up to the house. I can't believe she's wearing a dress like that to a party like this.

KEN   All right, what do we do? Do we tell them or not?

CLAIRE   Why not? Ernie is Charley's analyst. Everything you tell your analyst remains confidential.

LENNY   What his *patients* tell him. We're not his patients. His patient is asleep sucking his thumb.

CHRIS   I can't believe I'm paying a baby-sitter for this night.

(The doorbell rings. They all freeze)

LENNY   So what did we decide? Do we call the police or not?

CHRIS   I say no. Cookie has her cooking show on television. Suppose she accidentally says something on the air.

LENNY   On a cooking show? Do you think she gives out suicide recipes?

36

KEN I still think we say nothing till I find out what's happened. Better safe than sorry. Claire, open the door.

LENNY Chris, get us some drinks. Let's look like we're having fun.

> (CHRIS *rushes to the bar, gets drinks, and sits beside* LENNY *on the sofa*)

CLAIRE So what is it? We're telling Ernie but we're not telling Cookie?

LENNY *We're not telling either one of them!* I'm sorry we told you! (*The doorbell rings*) Just open the door!

KEN Claire, don't open it until I get upstairs. If Charley wakes up, maybe I can get the story from him.

> (KEN *dashes upstairs to* CHARLEY's *bedroom*)

CHRIS *(To* KEN) I took the Valium away from him. I hid them in the medicine cabinet.

KEN Gee, what a good hiding place.

> (KEN *exits into* CHARLEY's *room.* CLAIRE *goes to the front door.* LENNY *and* CHRIS *quickly sit on the sofa with their drinks as if they're having an amusing chat*)

LENNY *(To* CHRIS) So, Mrs. Thatcher replies, "I don't know, perhaps it's in my umbrella stand."

CLAIRE *(At the front door)* Are we ready?

LENNY Yes! We're ready, we're ready!

(CLAIRE *smiles and opens the front door.* CHRIS *and* LENNY *break into loud laughter.*
ERNIE *and* COOKIE *are at the door.* ERNIE *is in his early fifties and is wearing a tuxedo and carrying a gift box.* COOKIE *is in her forties and is wearing a god-awful evening gown. She is carrying a sausage-like cushion under her arm)*

CLAIRE Cookie! Ernie! It's so good to see you.

(CLAIRE *hugs them both)*

CHRIS Oh, God, that is so funny, Lenny. You should have been an actor, I swear.

CLAIRE Everybody, it's Ernie and Cookie.

LENNY *(Still laughing)* Hi, Ernie. Hi, Cookie.

CHRIS *(She waves, still laughing)* Hi, Cookie. Hi, Ernie.

ERNIE Hello, Chris. Hello, Lenny.

CHRIS *(To* LENNY*)* So go on with the story. What did Mr. Gorbachev say?

LENNY *(After an awkward silence)* Mr. Gorbachev? . . . He said, "I don't know. I never ate cat food before."

(There is much forced laughter)

ERNIE Sorry we're late. Did we miss much?

CHRIS   You have *got* to get Lenny to tell you the story about Mrs. Thatcher and the cat food.

(LENNY *shoots* CHRIS *a dirty look*)

ERNIE   *(He laughs)*   It sounds funny already. Heh heh heh.

COOKIE   Everyone looks so beautiful.

CLAIRE   Cookie, I am crazy about the dress. You always dig up the most original things. Where do you find them?

COOKIE   Oh, God, this is sixty years old. It was my grandmother's. She brought it from Russia.

CLAIRE   Didn't you wear that for Muscular Dystrophy in June?

COOKIE   No. Emphysema in August.

CLAIRE *(Looking at the cushion)*   Oh, what a pretty cushion. Is that for Charley and Myra?

COOKIE   No, it's for my back. It went out again while I was dressing.

(She opens the pretzels, easily)

ERNIE   You all right, honey?

COOKIE   I'm fine, babe.

CHRIS   You and your back problems. It must be awful.

COOKIE   It's nothing. I can do everything but sit down and get up.

ERNIE   Hey, Lenny, is that your BMW? *(He laughs)* Looks like you put a lot of miles on in two days.

LENNY   A guy shoots out of a garage and blindsides me. The car's got twelve miles on it. I've got a case of whiplash you wouldn't believe.

COOKIE *(Moving to the other side of the room)*   Oh, I've had whiplash. Excruciating. My best friend had it for six years. (LENNY *nods sardonically. She picks up the Steuben gift box)* Oh, this looks nice. Who brought this? *(She turns it to see the label but loses control and drops it)* Oh, my God . . . Did I break anything? *(She shakes the box. It rattles)* What was it?

LENNY   Steuben glass.

COOKIE   Oh, don't tell me! Lenny! Claire! . . . I'm so sorry.

ERNIE   It was an accident, honey. *(To* LENNY *and* CLAIRE*)* We'll replace it, of course.

LENNY   Sure, if you want. I don't care.

CHRIS   What about a drink, everyone?

ERNIE   I'll have something.

CHRIS   What do you want?

CLAIRE   I'll get it.

LENNY *(Getting up)* I'm right near the bar.

ERNIE You're all going to get me a drink? Such friendly people. I'd love a bourbon, please.

(CHRIS goes to the bar)

COOKIE I should have let what's her name pick it up. Moo Loo.

CHRIS Mai Li . . . Here you go, Ern. *(She gives ERNIE his drink)*

COOKIE Where's Ken?

CLAIRE Ken? Ken's with Charley.

COOKIE And Myra?

CLAIRE Myra's with Ken . . . They're waiting for Myra to get dressed.

COOKIE *(She grabs the back of a chair and screams)* Ooooh! Ooooh! Ooooh!

CLAIRE What is it?

COOKIE A spasm. It's gone. It's all right. It just shoots up my back and goes.

ERNIE You all right, Poops?

COOKIE I'm fine, puppy.

LENNY Listen, maybe we should all sit outside. It's such a beautiful evening.

ERNIE *(He smiles)*   Okay. Okay, you kids, what's going on here?

CLAIRE   What do you mean?

ERNIE   You think I don't notice everyone's acting funny? Three people want to get me drinks. Chris wants me to hear this funny story. Lenny wants to get us all outside. Everyone creating a diversion. Why? I don't know. Am I right?

CHRIS   No wonder you're such a high-priced doctor. Okay . . . Someone's going to have to tell them.

LENNY   Tell them what?

CHRIS   About the surprise.

LENNY   What surprise?

CHRIS   The surprise about the party.

COOKIE   What surprise about the party?

CHRIS   Well, I think it's the cutest thing, isn't it, Claire?

CLAIRE   Oh, God, yes.

CHRIS   Tell them about it.

CLAIRE   No, you tell it better than I do.

COOKIE   I'm sorry. I think I'm going to have to sit down.

CHRIS   I'll help you.

LENNY I'll do it.

CLAIRE I've got her.

> *(They all help lower* COOKIE *onto the sofa beside* ERNIE*)*

COOKIE The cushion. I need the cushion.

LENNY Here it is.

> *(He puts the cushion behind* COOKIE*'s back)*

ERNIE You all right, chicken?

COOKIE I'm fine, Poops . . . So what's the big surprise about?

CHRIS Well . . . Charley and Myra decided . . . because they were going to have their closest friends over to celebrate their tenth anniversary . . . they weren't going to have any . . . servants.

COOKIE *(She nods)* Uh huh.

CHRIS No Mai Li, no anybody.

COOKIE *(She nods)* Uh huh.

CHRIS Isn't that terrific? No help. Just us.

COOKIE Why is that terrific?

43

CHRIS   Because!! We're all going to pitch in. Like in the old days. Before money. Before success. Like when we were all just starting out. Those were the best times in our lives, don't you think?

COOKIE   No, I hated those times. I love success.

CHRIS   But don't you find these are greedier times? Lazier, more selfish. Nobody wants to work anymore.

COOKIE   I work fourteen hours a day. I cook thirty-seven meals a week. I cook on my television show. I cook for my family. I cook for my neighbors. I cook for my dogs. I was looking forward to a relaxed evening. *(She reconsiders)* But I don't want to spoil the fun. What do we have to do?

CLAIRE   We have to cook.

COOKIE   You mean all of us cooking in the kitchen together?

CHRIS   Everyone except Charley and Myra. Claire and I told them to stay up there and relax. We'll call them when we're ready.

COOKIE   What are we going to make?

CLAIRE   It's all laid out. Roast ham, smoked turkey, duck, and pasta.

ERNIE   Roast ham? Duck? . . . That's too much cholesterol for me.

LENNY   Ernie, we didn't come here to live longer. Just to have a good time.

COOKIE I just don't understand why we're all wearing our best clothes to cook a dinner.

CLAIRE That's not your best clothes. It's a fifty-year-old Polish dress.

COOKIE A sixty-year-old Russian dress.

ERNIE The dress is hardly an issue worth arguing about.

COOKIE I didn't say we wouldn't cook it.

ERNIE She didn't say we wouldn't cook it. Why is everyone getting so worked up about this?

CLAIRE All right, Ernie, let's not turn this into group therapy, please.

ERNIE This is nothing like group therapy, Claire. You, of all people, should know that.

LENNY Oh, terrific. Let's just name all the people in your Thursday night group, Ernie, heh?

COOKIE Why are Ernie and I being attacked? We just walked in the door.

CHRIS Please lower your voices. We're going to spoil the surprise for Charley and Myra.

ERNIE What surprise? It was their idea.

COOKIE Listen, I don't want to take the blame for ruining this party. *(To the group)* I'll do all the cooking myself and Ernie'll do the serving.

ERNIE   Honey, no one's asking you to do that.

CHRIS *and* CLAIRE   If she wants to do it, let her. Sure. Why not? Fine with us.

LENNY   If it makes her happy, she can clean up, too.

COOKIE *(Struggling to her feet)*   Okay, then it's settled. Just give me forty-five minutes. I promise you this is going to be the best dinner party we ever had. *(Suddenly, we hear a gunshot from* CHARLEY'*s room)* Oh, my God!

> *(Everyone freezes.* COOKIE *falls back onto the sofa)*

CLAIRE   Oh, give me a break.

ERNIE   What the hell was that?

> *(*CHARLEY'*s bedroom door opens and* KEN, *looking harassed, comes out, looks over the railing, and tries to appear calm)*

KEN   It's fine. It's okay. It's all under control. Hi, Ernie. Hi, Cookie . . . Oh, Chris, honey, could I see you up here for a minute . . .

> *(He smiles at them and returns to* CHARLEY'*s bedroom)*

CHRIS *(Politely)*   Would you all excuse me for a minute? I hate when this happens.

> *(She goes calmly up the stairs and into Charley's room)*

ERNIE   Am I crazy or was that a gunshot?

LENNY   A gunshot? Nooo. I think it was a car backfiring.

ERNIE   In Charley's bedroom?

COOKIE   Ernie, maybe you should go up and see.

LENNY   Why? Chris and Ken and Charley and Myra are up there. There's more of them than us.

COOKIE   You just can't ignore a gunshot. Ernie, please go up and see.

LENNY   Oh, I know. I know. I know exactly what it was . . . It was a balloon. They've been blowing up party balloons up there all day.

ERNIE   What kind of a balloon was that, the Goodyear Blimp? . . . I'm going up.

LENNY   Then how are we going to get the dinner ready? Charley and Myra must be starved. You and Cookie get started. I'll have a white wine spritzer, Ern. Claire, why don't you put on some music? *(Rushing upstairs)* I'll be right down. Let me know if Dr. Doolittle calls.

> *(He disappears into* CHARLEY's *bedroom. The telephone rings)*

CLAIRE   I'll get it.

> *(She goes to the phone)*

ERNIE   I still think it sounded like a gunshot.

COOKIE   Let's get dinner started, Ern. Help me up.

(She tries to get up out of the sofa)

CLAIRE *(Into the phone)*   Hello? . . . Who? Dr. Cusack? Yes, he is. Who is it, please?

ERNIE *(To CLAIRE)*   Is that for me?

CLAIRE *(Into the phone)*   Uh huh. Uh huh. *(To ERNIE)* It's a conference call. Mr. and Mrs. Klein, Mr. and Mrs. Platt, Mr. and Mrs. Fishman.

ERNIE   Oh, it's my Friday night group. I have a telephone session with them.

COOKIE   Go on, honey. I can get up myself.

(ERNIE runs into the kitchen)

CLAIRE *(Into the phone)*   He's coming, folks. *(The other line on the phone rings. She switches buttons)* Hello? . . . Yes it is. No, my husband just called. (COOKIE *gets down on the floor and crawls on her hands and knees)* Yes, I'll tell him.

(She holds the phone. LENNY comes out of CHARLEY's room)

LENNY   Who's on the phone?

CLAIRE   Dr. Dudley's service.

LENNY *(He nods and comes downstairs. He sees COOKIE crawling on the floor)*   Oh, my God. What's that?

CLAIRE   It's Cookie.

COOKIE   It's all right. I do this all the time. It takes the pressure off my back.

LENNY   Where's Ernie?

CLAIRE *(Pointing toward the kitchen)*   In there. He's got a session with his Friday night group.

LENNY   They're all in the kitchen?

CLAIRE   No. On the telephone.

COOKIE *(Crawling toward the dining room)*   Ah! Ah! Ah!

LENNY   Your back again?

COOKIE   No. Little shirt pins on the floor. *(She crawls off into the kitchen)* Ah! Ah! Ah!

LENNY *(To CLAIRE)*   She must be such fun to live with.

CLAIRE   What happened upstairs? Is Charley all right?

LENNY   He was sleeping. Ken wanted to hide the gun in the closet so Charley wouldn't find it. He tripped on Charley's slippers and the gun went off next to his head. He can't hear a thing in both ears.

CLAIRE   Ken or Charley?

LENNY   Ken. Charley was out cold from the Valium.

(He sees the phone is hung up)

CLAIRE   They hung up. I already took the message.

LENNY   You couldn't tell me that while I was on the balcony? What'd they say?

CLAIRE   They said Dr. Dudley already called this number. He doesn't want to be called out of the theater again.

LENNY *(He angrily redials the phone)*   I'm getting a new doctor. I'm not putting my life in the hands of the drama critic for Mount Sinai Hospital. *(Into the phone)* Hello? This is Leonard Ganz again. Dr. Dudley did *not* call this number. Please have him call me back. It's important.

   (He hangs up the phone)

CLAIRE   So what did Ken want Chris upstairs for?

LENNY   To call Ken's doctor to ask him what to do for his ears. He wouldn't be able to hear what the doctor was saying on the phone. I've got to get back upstairs.

   (He starts back upstairs)

CLAIRE   You mean she told the doctor a gun went off? Then she'll have to explain about Charley.

LENNY   No. She was going to say Ken was outside and a manhole cover blew up next to him.

CLAIRE   That's a good idea.

LENNY   Except the doctor wasn't in. His service said he was still at the theater. There must be some kind of flu going around on Broadway. *(He runs upstairs. When he hits the top step, the phone rings)* They purposely wait till I get on top of the stairs. Answer that, will you?

CLAIRE *(Going to the phone)* This is all too hard to follow. I need a bookmark in my head or something. *(She picks up the phone)* Hello? Oh, Dr. Dudley, thanks for calling back. *(To LENNY)* You want to speak to him?

LENNY *(Running down the stairs)* No. I'm taking a stress test.

CLAIRE You know, if Ernie can't figure out something's wrong here, I'm not going to his group anymore.

LENNY *(Picking up the phone)* Hello, Dr. Dudley? . . . Thanks for calling back . . . Well, some idiot nailed me in my BMW about twenty minutes ago. I've got a little whiplash here . . . Charley? Charley Brock? . . . No, I wasn't calling about Charley. Why? *(Covering the phone, to CLAIRE)* Jesus! Dr. Dudley is Charley's doctor, too. *(Into the phone)* No, Charley's a lot better. He's resting now . . . Chris Gorman? You know Ken and Chris? Yes, I think she did call. *(Covering the phone, to CLAIRE)* He's Ken's doctor, too.

CLAIRE Maybe he has a franchise.

LENNY Will you make yourself busy? Put on some music. *(Into the phone)* Dr. Dudley? I'm sorry. A cold compress? . . . Good idea. Let me connect you to Chris. Hold on. *(He presses the "Hold" button, then looks at the extension numbers)* Which button rings in Charley's room?

CLAIRE Why? Who's going to hear it up there?

LENNY *(Not covering the phone)* Jesus, you are a pain in the ass. Dr. Dudley? . . . What? . . . Oh, yes, my wife has a pain, too. It's no bother. Can you hold for Chris, please? *(He puts the phone on hold, then dashes upstairs)* We owe this guy a gift. Let's give him Cookie as a patient. See where Ernie is with my drink, will you?

(He goes into CHARLEY'*s bedroom. The dining room door opens and* ERNIE *comes out with a drink)*

ERNIE I thought I heard Lenny in here. I have his spritzer.

CLAIRE I'll hold it for him. How's Cookie?

(She takes the drink)

ERNIE Not well. I gave her some aspirin for her back, but she dropped them in the sauce.

CLAIRE Good. Then we'll all get rid of *our* headaches.

ERNIE Did Lenny say what that sound was?

CLAIRE The gunshot?

ERNIE It *was* a gunshot?

CLAIRE No, I was referring to the sound you *thought* was a gunshot.

ERNIE It wasn't a balloon, I know that.

CLAIRE No. It was a can of shaving cream. It exploded.

ERNIE Shaving cream exploded?

CLAIRE   It's all right. It washes off.

ERNIE   Incredible.

COOKIE *(Sticking her head out the dining room door)*
Ernie? I need you to put out some garbage.

ERNIE   I'm not through talking to my group yet.

COOKIE   They're fighting with each other. I put them on
hold.

> (COOKIE *and* ERNIE *exit into the kitchen.* CHARLEY'S
> *bedroom door opens and* LENNY *and* KEN *come out.*
> KEN *holds a towel over his ears)*

LENNY   It'll clear up in a minute. These things don't last
long.

KEN   You think this'll last long?

LENNY *(Opening the guest room door)*   Lie down in the
guest room for a while, Ken. You'll feel better.

KEN *(Looking into the guest room)*   Maybe if I lie down
in the guest room for a while . . .

LENNY   Right.

CLAIRE *(To* LENNY*)*   What did the doctor say to Chris?

LENNY   He referred her to another doctor. He's not feeling well himself . . . My neck is killing me again.
Where's my spritzer?

KEN *(Coming out of the guest room, to* LENNY*)*   Is your sister here?

LENNY   No, my *spritzer!!* Come on, Ken. I'll heat that towel up again.

KEN   Don't tell your sister about Charley. Not till we hear the whole story.

>   *(They go into the guest room. The kitchen door opens and* COOKIE *comes out. She holds a ladle in one hand and with her other hand supports a bag of ice on her hip)*

COOKIE   I've got a problem, Claire, can you help me? Ernie went out the kitchen door to put out some garbage bags and the door locked. My hands are full of grease. Could you let him back in?

CLAIRE   Of course. We would all miss him terribly.

>   *(*CLAIRE *leaves and goes into the kitchen.* ERNIE *enters the house through the front door)*

ERNIE   I purposely went around so you wouldn't have to go to the door.

>   *(*CHARLEY*'s bedroom door opens and* CHRIS *steps out)*

CHRIS   Oh, hi! . . . Where's Claire?

COOKIE   She went out to the kitchen to let Ernie in.

CHRIS *(Looking at* ERNIE*)*   Oh. Okay.

> *(She smiles and goes back into* CHARLEY*'s bedroom, closing the door. The dining room door opens and* CLAIRE *comes out)*

CLAIRE   Oh, there you are . . . Cookie, the water's boiling over on the pasta.

COOKIE   Why didn't you turn it down?

CLAIRE   I don't know. I don't watch your show.

COOKIE   I'll get it. Ernie, get another bag of ice. I'm melting.

> *(*COOKIE *leaves and goes into the kitchen)*

ERNIE *(Following* COOKIE, *to* CLAIRE*)*   I'm beginning to feel like one of my patients.

> *(He laughs and goes to the kitchen.* CHARLEY*'s door opens and* CHRIS *comes out)*

CHRIS *(With a big smile)*   Well, everything is just fine.

CLAIRE   It's all right. They're in the kitchen.

CHRIS   God, I'd smoke a Havana cigar if I had one. *(She comes downstairs, scratching herself under her arms)* I'm getting hives under my arms. *(She goes to the bar and makes herself a vodka)* Did you hear about Ken? He's deaf.

CLAIRE   He's better off. He's out of this thing now.

CHRIS   Why are we protecting Charley this way? Ken is deaf, Lenny can't turn his neck, Cookie's walking like a giraffe, I'm getting a blood condition. *(She scratches under her arms again)* For what? One more gunshot, the whole world will know anyway.

CLAIRE   The whole world isn't interested. Paraguay and Bolivia don't give a rat's ass.

(We hear another car coming up the driveway)

LENNY   *(Coming out of the guest room)*   There's another car coming up. *(We see the headlights flash on the window)* Was anyone else invited?

CHRIS   Harry and Joan, but they canceled. They went to Venezuela. But they said they'd call tonight.

LENNY   From Venezuela?

CLAIRE   Jeez, maybe they *will* hear about it in Bolivia.

LENNY   So who's coming up the driveway?

CHRIS   Maybe it's Myra. Maybe she's come back.

LENNY   Myra drives a Porsche. This is an Audi.

(He comes halfway down the stairs)

CLAIRE   Ask Ken. He might know.

LENNY   Ken is reading lips right now. I don't think he can pick up on "Audi." *(We hear a loud crash from the kitchen)* Jesus, what the hell was that?

CHRIS Cookie just blew up the microwave, what else?

LENNY Chris, go inside and see what happened. Claire, go to the window and see who's coming. I'll go up and see how Ken and Charley are doing . . . *(He has been gesturing with a white towel)* I feel like I'm at the fucking Alamo.

(He rushes upstairs, just as the dining room door flies open and ERNIE *comes out, flicking his fingers in pain)*

ERNIE Damn, I burned my fingers! Hot hot hot, oh, *God,* it's hot!

CHRIS Oh, dear.

ERNIE Sonofagun, that hurts. Oh, fuckerini!

CLAIRE What happened?

ERNIE *(Quickly)* Cookie dropped her ice bag and slipped against the stove. The hot platter was about to fall on her, so I lifted it up. Then I dropped it on the table and it broke the water pitcher and the glass shattered on her arm and she's bleeding like hell. I got a dish towel on her wrist and I propped her up against a cabinet. But I need some bandages for her arm and some ointment for my fingers. I never saw anything happen so fast.

LENNY I can't believe he's in pain and said all that without missing a word.

CLAIRE *(To* LENNY*)* Get the bandages. Why are you standing there?

LENNY   I was hoping there was more to the story.

> *(He rushes into* CHARLEY's *room and closes the door)*

ERNIE   I'm sorry, Claire. Did you ask for a drink?

CLAIRE   Listen, you have other things to think about.

ERNIE   Right.

> *(He leaves.* CHRIS *and* CLAIRE *stare at each other)*

CLAIRE   You know what this night is beginning to re-mind me of? . . . *Platoon.*

> *(A car door slams outside)*

CHRIS   There's the car. I don't even want to know who it is. Why don't you go and look?

CLAIRE   Like it's going to be good news, right? *(She goes to the window and looks out)* It's Glenn and Cassie.

CHRIS   Glenn and Cassie Cooper? Together?

CLAIRE   That's how they're walking.

CHRIS   I heard they were having trouble.

CLAIRE   Not walking.

> *(She comes away from the window)*

CHRIS   Jesus! Do you know that Glenn is running for state senate in Poughkeepsie.

CLAIRE   So?

CHRIS   That's all he needs is to walk in here and be part of a hushed-up suicide attempt. He can kiss his career good-bye.

CLAIRE   Maybe Ken'll figure this all out before they ring the doorbell. *(The doorbell rings)* Well, it's going to be a tough campaign.

CHRIS   Listen, I have to go to the bathroom. You get the door, I'll be right out.

(She starts for the powder room)

CLAIRE   Wait a minute! I haven't gone since I got here.

CHRIS   Yes you did. In Mai Li's room.

CLAIRE   Yes, but no one was at the door then.

CHRIS   The hell with it. Someone else'll get the door. Come on.

(They both go into the powder room and close the door behind them. The doorbell rings again. LENNY *comes out of the guest room)*

LENNY   Isn't anybody going to get the door? . . . Chris? . . . Claire? . . .

KEN *(Peering out from the guest room)*   Are you talking to me?

59

LENNY   No, Ken. Put the towels back on your ears. *(Yelling down)* Claire? . . . Chris? . . . Where are you? . . . Ah, screw it. I'm beginning to feel like my car.

> *(He goes back into the guest room and closes the door. The dining room door opens and* ERNIE *comes out with paper towels wrapped around all his fingers. He is wearing an apron. He shouts up)*

ERNIE   Lenny? You got those bandages? *(The doorbell rings again)* Nobody getting that door? . . . These kids are up to something, I know it. *(He goes to the front door and tries to open it with burned fingers. He is finally successful.* GLENN *and* CASSIE COOPER, *a handsome couple, stand there in evening clothes.* GLENN *holds a gift from Ralph Lauren's. They seem very much on edge with each other.* ERNIE *smiles)* Hello.

GLENN   Good evening.

> *(They walk in and look around.* ERNIE *closes the door with his foot)*

ERNIE   Good evening. I don't know where everyone is.

CASSIE   You mean we're the first?

ERNIE   No. Everyone's here. They're just—spread out a little.

GLENN   Could I have a drink, please? Double scotch, straight up.

CASSIE *(Not looking at* ERNIE*)*   Perrier with lime, no ice.

ERNIE   Sure. Fine. I don't believe we've met. I'm Ernie Cusack.

GLENN *(He coolly nods)*   Hello, Ernie.

ERNIE   Excuse my hands. Little accident in the kitchen.

GLENN   Sorry to hear it.

ERNIE   I would stay and chat but my wife is bleeding in the kitchen.

GLENN   Your wife?

ERNIE   Cookie. A water pitcher broke, cut her arm. I burned my fingers.

GLENN   That's a shame.

ERNIE   Nothing to worry about. We'll have dinner ready soon. Nice meeting you both.

    (He returns to the kitchen)

GLENN   I wonder why they're not using the Chinese girl?

CASSIE   Do I look all right?

GLENN   Yes. Fine.

CASSIE   I feel so frumpy.

GLENN   God, no. You look beautiful.

CASSIE   My hair isn't right, is it? I saw you looking at it in the car.

GLENN   No, I wasn't.

CASSIE   What were you looking at then?

GLENN   The road, I suppose.

CASSIE   I can always tell when you hate what I'm wearing.

GLENN   I love that dress. I always have.

CASSIE   This is the first time I've worn it.

GLENN   I always have admired your taste is what I meant.

CASSIE   It's so hard to please you sometimes.

GLENN   What did I say?

CASSIE   It's what you *don't* say that really drives me crazy.

GLENN   What I *don't* say? . . . How can it drive you crazy if I don't say it?

CASSIE   I don't know. It's the looks that you give me.

GLENN   I wasn't giving you any looks.

CASSIE   You look at me all the time.

GLENN   Because you're always asking me to look at you.

CASSIE   It would be nice if I didn't have to ask you, wouldn't it?

GLENN   It would be nice if you didn't need me to look, which would make it unnecessary to ask.

CASSIE   I can't ever get any support from you. You've got all the time in the world for everything and everyone else, but I've got to draw blood to get your attention when I walk in a room.

GLENN   We walked in together. It was already done. Cassie, please don't start. We're forty-five minutes late as it is. I don't want to ruin this night for Charley and Myra.

CASSIE   We're forty-five minutes late because you scowled at every dress I tried on.

GLENN   I didn't scowl, I smiled. You always think my smile looks like a scowl. You think my grin looks like a frown, and my frown looks like a yawn.

CASSIE   Don't sneer at me.

GLENN   It wasn't a sneer. It was a peeve.

CASSIE   God, this conversation is so banal. I can't believe any of the things I'm saying. We sound like some fucking TV couple.

GLENN   Oh, now we're going to get into language, right?

CASSIE   No, Mr. Perfect. No language. I don't want to risk a scowl, a frown, a yawn, a peeve, or a sneer. God forbid I should show a human imperfection, I'd wake up with the divorce papers in my hand.

GLENN   What is this thing lately with divorce? Where does that come from? I don't look at you sometimes because I'm afraid you're thinking you don't like the way I'm looking at you.

CASSIE   I don't know what the hell you want from me, Glenn. I really don't.

GLENN   I don't want *any*thing from you. I mean I would like it to be the way we were before we got to be the way we are.

CASSIE   God, you suffocate me sometimes . . . I want to go home.

GLENN   Go home? We just got here. We haven't even seen anyone yet.

CASSIE   I don't know how I'm going to get through this night. They all know what's going on. They're your friends. Jesus, and you expect me to behave like nothing's happening.

GLENN   Nothing is happening. What are you talking about?

CASSIE   Don't you fucking lie to me. The whole goddamn city knows about you and that cheap little chippy bimbo.

GLENN Will you keep it down? Nothing is going on. You're blowing this up out of all proportion. I hardly know the woman. She's on the Democratic Fund-raising Committee. I met her and her husband at two cocktail parties, for God's sakes.

CASSIE Two cocktail parties, heh?

GLENN Yes! Two cocktail parties.

CASSIE You think I'm stupid?

GLENN No.

CASSIE You think I'm blind?

GLENN No.

CASSIE You think I don't know what's been going on?

GLENN Yes, because you don't.

CASSIE I'm going to tell you something, Glenn. Are you listening?

GLENN Don't you see my ears perking up?

CASSIE I've known about you and Carole Newman for a year now.

GLENN Amazing, since I only met her four months ago. Now I'm asking you to please lower your voice. That butler must be listening to everything.

CASSIE You think I care about a butler and a bleeding cook? My friends know about your bimbo, what do I care about domestic help?

GLENN I don't know what's gotten into you, Cassie. Do my political ambitions bother you? Are you threatened somehow because I'm running for the senate?

CASSIE *State* senate! *State* senate! Don't make it sound like we're going to Washington. We're going to Albany. Twenty-three degrees below zero in the middle of winter Albany. You're not *Time*'s Man of the Year yet, you understand, honey?

GLENN *(Turning away)* Oh boy, oh boy, oh boy!

CASSIE What was that?

GLENN *(Deliberately)* Oh-boy, oh-boy, oh-boy!

CASSIE Oh, like I'm behaving badly, right? I'm the shrew witch wife who's giving you such a hard time. I'll tell you something, Mr. *State* Senator. I'm not the only one who knows what's going on. People are talking, kiddo. Trust me.

GLENN What do you mean? You haven't said anything to anyone, have you?

CASSIE Oh, is that what you're worried about? Your reputation? Your career? Your place in American history? You know what your place in American history will be? . . . A commemorative stamp of you and the bimbo in a motel together.

GLENN   You are so hyper tonight, Cassie. You're out of control. You've been rubbing your quartz crystal again, haven't you? I told you to throw those damn crystals away. They're dangerous. They're like petrified cocaine. (CASSIE *is looking through her purse*) . . . Don't take it out, Cassie. Don't rub your crystal at the party. It makes you crazy. *(She takes out her crystal. He grabs for it)* Put it away. Don't let my friends see what you're doing.

CASSIE   Fine. Don't let *my* friends see what *you're* doing.

> *(The guest room door opens.* LENNY *comes out onto the balcony)*

LENNY   Glenn! Cassie! I thought it was you. How you doing?

KEN *(From inside the guest room)*   I'm feeling better, thanks.

LENNY   Not you, Ken. It's Glenn and Cassie.

GLENN *(With a big smile)*   We're fine. Just great. Hi, Len . . . Cassie, it's Len . . . Cassie.

CASSIE *(With a quick nod)*   Leonard.

LENNY   Did it suddenly freeze up out there?

GLENN   Freeze up?

LENNY   Isn't that an icicle Cassie has there?

GLENN   No. It's a quartz crystal.

67

LENNY   Oh. Where's Chris and Claire?

KEN *(From the guest room)*   Did somebody come in?

LENNY *(Angrily, to* KEN*)*   GLENN AND CASSIE!! I *TOLD* YOU!! *(To* GLENN*)* It's Ken. His ears are stuffed up. Bad cold . . . Who let you in?

GLENN   The butler.

LENNY   The butler? The butler's here?

GLENN   He's getting us drinks.

LENNY   Is he alone?

GLENN   No, the cook's with him.

LENNY   Mai Li? God, what a relief. They came back. We didn't have any help here for a while.

GLENN   Really? Where's Charley and Myra?

LENNY   Charley and Myra? I guess they're in their room.

KEN *(From the guest room)*   My towel fell off, Lenny.

LENNY *(Angrily, to* KEN*)*   I'LL GET YOU A TOWEL. I'VE GOT TO GET THE BANDAGES FIRST. *(To* GLENN*)* Excuse me, kids. I've got to get some bandages. *(He knocks on* CHARLEY's *door)* Charley? Myra? Is it all right if I come in? *(In* MYRA's *voice)* Sure, come on in.

> *(He goes into* CHARLEY's *room and closes the door. The guest room door opens and* KEN *comes out)*

KEN   Lenny? . . . Lenny, where'd you go? *(GLENN and CASSIE look up)*

GLENN   Ken? Hi. It's Glenn and Cassie.

KEN   Lenny? Is that you? *(He looks down)* Who's that? Glenn? Is that Glenn?

GLENN   Yes. And Cassie. I hear you have a cold.

KEN   You think I look old? I haven't been sleeping well lately . . . Hi, Cassie. Do the others know you're here?

GLENN   Yes. We just saw Lenny.

KEN   Have you seen Lenny?

GLENN   Yes. He went into Charley's room.

KEN   I'm sorry. I can't hear anything. A manhole cover just blew up next to my ear.

GLENN   That's terrible.

KEN   I said, a manhole cover just blew up next to my ear.

GLENN   Yes. I hear you.

KEN   I'm sorry. I can't hear you. Anyone getting you a drink?

GLENN   Yes, the butler.

KEN   Sorry, there's no help here. They're in the Orient somewhere.

CASSIE *(To* GLENN*)*   I think he's gone dotty.

KEN   Yes, a hot toddy would be nice. I'm going to see if Lenny's in Charley's room. We're all coming down soon. *(He knocks on* CHARLEY*'s door)* Myra? Mind if I come in?

LENNY *(As* MYRA, *from inside)*   Sure, honey. Come on in.

*(*KEN *goes into* CHARLEY*'s room)*

CASSIE   I'll be right back.

GLENN   Where are you going?

CASSIE   To rinse off my crystal. *(Going to the powder room)* . . . I suppose you'd like to make a *quick* phone call while I'm gone, heh? *(She tries to open the powder room door, but it's locked)* Anyone in there?

CHRIS *(From inside)*   Who is it?

CASSIE   Cassie. Who's that?

CHRIS *(From inside)*   It's Chris . . . Just a minute, Cass. *(We hear a flush.* CHRIS *comes out and closes the door)* I didn't hear you ring, Cassie. I would have opened the door. Hi, Glenn.

(She goes over to him and gives him a kiss. By now she's getting pretty crocked from her vodkas)

GLENN   Hi. Listen, is anything going on here?

CHRIS   I don't know . . . Who have you seen?

GLENN   Well, Lenny and Ken for just a second. And the butler and Mai Li.

CHRIS   You saw Mai Li and the butler? My God, I must have been in there for a long time.

CASSIE   Are you through in the bathroom?

CHRIS   Me? Yes. Sure.

(CASSIE *tries the door again, but it's locked*)

CASSIE   You left it locked.

CLAIRE *(From inside)*   Who is it?

CASSIE   Cassie. Who's that?

CLAIRE *(From inside)*   It's Claire. Just a minute, Cass. *(We hear a flush. The door opens and* CLAIRE *comes out)* Hi, Cass. Hi, Glenn. Don't you look beautiful . . . Where are the boys?

GLENN   Well, Lenny and Ken are up with Charley and Myra. Myra sounded very excited.

CLAIRE   You spoke to Myra?

GLENN   No. I heard her talk to Ken and Len.

CLAIRE   I'd love to have a copy of that conversation.

CASSIE   Is anyone else in the bathroom, because I have to go.

(She looks inside, then goes in and locks the door behind her)

CHRIS *(To* CLAIRE*)*   Mai Li and the butler are here.

CLAIRE You're kidding. Where's Ernie and Cookie?

GLENN I just met Ernie. Isn't he the butler?

CHRIS Oh. No. Okay. We've got that one cleared up.

GLENN Then they're just back from the Orient?

CHRIS I imagine so. You're so well informed.

GLENN Why is everyone up in Charley's room?

CHRIS Oh. There was something on TV they all wanted to watch.

CLAIRE Right. Very good, Chris. (CHARLEY's *bedroom door opens, and* LENNY *comes out*)

LENNY (*Jovially*) Well, this is beginning to look like a party.

GLENN What were you all watching up there?

LENNY Up where?

GLENN On TV.

CHRIS (*To* LENNY) The thing you went up to watch with Ken and Charley and Myra.

LENNY Oh. Oh! *That thing. That show. That PBS special on what's-his-name?*

CLAIRE . . . Hitler?

LENNY   Yes. The thing on Hitler.

(He comes downstairs, glaring at CLAIRE)

GLENN   On their tenth anniversary you wanted to watch a special on Hitler?

LENNY   Hitler as a boy. A whole new slant on him.

(ERNIE *comes out of the dining room door. He is carrying two drinks)*

ERNIE   Dinner's coming along. *(To* GLENN) Double scotch, straight up.

GLENN   Oh, thanks.

ERNIE   Lenny, have you got the bandages?

LENNY   The bandages? Yes. I have them. I left them on Hitler . . . on the television. I'll be right back.

(He runs back upstairs and into CHARLEY's *room, closing the door behind him)*

GLENN   Listen, I'm sorry. I mistook you for the butler.

ERNIE   I kind of thought you did. No, I'm an analyst.

GLENN   Oh, for Pete sakes. I'm Glenn . . . How's your wife doing?

ERNIE   The spaghetti's boiling, but the duck is still frozen.

GLENN   No, I meant her arm.

ERNIE   Oh, not too bad. She's a trouper. Her fingers are cramping up a little.

GLENN   Maybe she ought to see a doctor. Charley has one ten minutes from here, Dr. Dudley.

CHRIS   Oh. We called him. He's busy.

ERNIE   You called about Cookie's arm?

CLAIRE   No, about Lenny's neck.

GLENN   Lenny's neck?

CHRIS   And when the doctor called back, we told him about Ken's ears.

ERNIE *(To GLENN)*   Isn't that incredible? From a can of shaving cream exploding?

GLENN   I thought it was a manhole cover.

CLAIRE   It was. But the pressure from the manhole cover made the shaving-cream can explode.

ERNIE *(To GLENN)*   I didn't hear that.

LENNY *(Coming out of CHARLEY's room with the bandages. He runs downstairs)*   I got 'em. I got 'em.

GLENN   There certainly is some excitement around here.

CLAIRE *(To LENNY)*   Guess who Glenn's doctor is?

LENNY   You're kidding. I wish I did his taxes.

ERNIE   Wait a minute! Glenn Cooper! From Pough-keepsie. You're running for the state senate.

GLENN   That's right.

ERNIE   I have a good friend who knows you very well.

GLENN   Really? Who's that?

ERNIE   Harold Green.

LENNY   Harold Green!

(LENNY *drops the bandages*)

CLAIRE   Harold Green?

GLENN   Sure. I know Harold Green. We went to the University of Pennsylvania together. I haven't seen him in years. What's he doing now?

LENNY   He's a proxy new social member who just eats lunches and doesn't play tennis.

GLENN   Oh. At your club?

(GLENN *hands the bandages to* ERNIE)

LENNY   Ernie, Cookie's waiting in the emergency room.

ERNIE   Right. *(To* GLENN*)* There's your wife's Perrier. Nice to meet you, Glenn. *(As he leaves to go to kitchen)* . . . Thought I was the butler.

(CHARLEY's *door opens and* KEN *comes out*)

KEN   Somebody! Please! I need a drink real bad.

GLENN   How's your ears, Ken?

KEN *(Coming downstairs)*   A beer would be fine, thanks.

GLENN   Maybe Charley has some ear drops. *(To* LENNY*)* Did you see any in the medicine cabinet when you were getting the bandages?

LENNY   No, I didn't think of that.

GLENN   I'll go up and look.

        (He starts up the stairs. LENNY *and* KEN *block him)*

LENNY   No. I remember. I looked. There weren't any. I forgot I looked.

        (The telephone rings)

KEN   Is there a cat in here?

CHRIS   A cat?

KEN   I just heard a cat meow. *(The telephone rings again)* There it is again.

GLENN   That's the *phone*, Ken.

KEN   Why would he want a bone? It's a cat, not a dog.

        (The telephone rings again)

LENNY   I'll get it.

KEN We're hungry, too, pussy. We haven't eaten either.

LENNY *(Into the phone)* Hello? . . . Who? . . . I'm sorry, operator. We have a bad connection . . . Oh, yes. Yes. *(To the others)* It's Harry and Joan from Venezuela. They're calling Charley and Myra.

CLAIRE This is going to be good.

GLENN Joan? That's Cassie's cousin. Wait, I'll get Cassie. I'm sure she'll want to speak to her. *(He knocks on the powder room door)* Cassie?

LENNY *(Into the phone)* Hello, Joannie. It's Lenny. How are you? . . . Yes, everybody's here . . . Yes, we're having a great time . . .

GLENN Cassie?

LENNY *(Into the phone)* Charley and Myra? Of course they're here. What did you think? *(He laughs and motions for CLAIRE and CHRIS to laugh, too)* Sure. Just a minute. *(Covering the phone)* Claire! Speak to her.

CLAIRE Me? She's calling Charley and Myra.

LENNY *Will you speak to her!!*

(He shoves the phone at Claire)

GLENN *(Knocking on the powder room door)* Cassie? It's your cousin Joan from Venezuela.

CLAIRE *(Into the phone)* Joan? What a nice surprise. No, it's Claire . . . Myra? Oh, she looks beautiful. She's

wearing a red kimono. Mai Li's mother sent it to her
... Wait, I'll let you speak to her. Hold on. *(Covering the phone, to* CHRIS*)* Here. Talk to her.

CHRIS Don't give me the phone. I'll drive your kids to school for a year.

CLAIRE *(Dumping the phone in* CHRIS*'s lap)* I've done my part. I'm not the Red Cross.

GLENN *(Knocking on the powder room door)* Cassie? It's Joan and Harry. Don't you want to speak to them?

CHRIS *(Into the phone)* Joan? Hi, sweetheart. How's Venezuela? ... No, it's Chris. You sent a gift? A crystal vase from Steuben's? Gee, I think it's broken. Wait, Myra will tell you about it.

GLENN *(Still knocking)* Cassie, are you all right?

CHRIS Who didn't speak to her yet?

CLAIRE Ken. Ken didn't speak to her.

LENNY *(Shouting at* KEN*, on the balcony)* Ken? Do you want to speak to Joan?

KEN What?

LENNY *Joan! Do-you-want-to-speak-to-Joan?*

KEN Sure. I'd love to go home.

CHRIS *(Into the phone)* Joan? This connection is bad. I think I'm losing you.

GLENN *(Banging on the bathroom door)* Cassie, will you hurry up! We're losing the connection! *Come on, will you!!*

> *(ERNIE and COOKIE come out of the kitchen. She is holding a hot casserole, he is holding two bottles of wine)*

COOKIE It's din-din, everyone.

> *(The bathroom door opens and CASSIE comes out in a state of shock)*

CASSIE *Who did that? Who banged on the door?*

GLENN I did. Your cousin Joan is on the phone from Venezuela.

CASSIE You scared the life out of me! I dropped my crystal down the toilet. A TWO-MILLION-YEAR-OLD CRYSTAL!!

CHRIS I can't take this. *(She shoves the phone into KEN's hand)* Here. You can't hear anyway, what's the difference?

> *(KEN holds the phone, bewildered. As CHRIS walks away, she trips on the phone cord and falls flat on her face)*

CASSIE *(To GLENN)* Don't just stand there, idiot, get my crystal.

GLENN Hey, just cool it, Cassie, okay?

KEN *(Into the phone)*   Hello? . . . Hello?

ERNIE *(Starting up the stairs)*   I'll go get Myra and Charley.

LENNY *(Dashing up the stairs, cutting off* ERNIE*)*   No, I'll get them, I'll get them. Myra and Charley! Myra and Chaaaaa . . . *(He grabs his neck)* Oh, shit! There it goes. This time it's permanent.

KEN   Hello? . . . Hello? . . .

CASSIE *(Crying)*   It's a sin to lose a crystal. It's like killing your own dog.

LENNY   Oh, fuck a duck!

COOKIE   Everybody grab a plate, kids. *(As she hands out plates, her back goes out)* Woops. Oh, no. Oh, Christ. Oh, man. Oh, Momma.

KEN   Hello? . . . Hello? . . .
                              Curtain

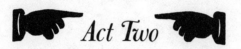

Act Two

One hour later.

Plates of eaten food are about. Opened wine and champagne bottles are scattered about.

It's quiet. Very quiet.

The only sound is of KEN *eating. He sits in an armchair finishing his dinner. The others have all eaten.* GLENN *and* CLAIRE *are seated on the sofa.* LENNY *is on the love seat, drinking wine.* COOKIE *sits on a chair near* KEN, *drinking coffee.* CASSIE *is standing on the balcony, holding the railing with her hands and drawing in deep breaths.* ERNIE *and* CHRIS *sit on the stairway.*

No one is talking. They are all deep in thought. No one looks at one another.

The silence continues.

KEN's *fork scratches on his plate as he eats the last morsel of food. He looks up.*

KEN *(Panicky)* What was that?

GLENN It was you, Ken. It was your fork scraping the plate.

KEN My what?

CHRIS Your fork scraping your plate.

KEN *(To* GLENN*)* You're fading out again, Glenn.

GLENN That wasn't me, Ken. It was Chris.

KEN I can make out voices now. Just a little here and there.

CHRIS *(To* ERNIE*)* You think I can have another cigarette?

KEN   No. No cigarettes.

GLENN *(Going over to* LENNY *at the love seat)*   I still can't get over it. I find the entire story so hard to believe.

LENNY   He finds the story hard to believe. Because we acted our asses off to keep the truth from you.

GLENN   Myra is gone?

LENNY   Right.

GLENN   The servants are gone?

LENNY   Right.

GLENN   Charley shoots himself in the earlobe?

LENNY   Right.

GLENN   It doesn't make any sense.

CLAIRE, CHRIS, *and* LENNY   Right!

ERNIE   Why didn't I see it? People running up and down stairs, no one answering a door, cans of shaving cream exploding. I'm on the staff of Bellevue Hospital, how could I believe such a story? *(To* CHRIS*)* You never let on.

CHRIS   Listen, I was so desperate for a smoke, I went into Charley's bathroom and tried to light up a Q-Tip.

COOKIE   Don't you have any self-control?

CHRIS Of course. I only smoked half. *(KEN suddenly stands and looks around at everyone. He is breathing hard and clenching his fists. He looks as though he's about to explode)* Something's wrong with Ken.

COOKIE Maybe he's still hungry. YOU WANT SEC-ONDS, KENNY?

ERNIE No, no. He wants to say something. Be quiet a minute, everyone . . . What is it, Ken?

KEN I can't take it anymore . . . The pressure is killing me. I'm sorry, but I have to do this. *(To ERNIE and GLENN)* Myra isn't here! The servants aren't here! Charley's upstairs and he shot himself through the ear-lobe! Maybe it was attempted suicide, maybe it wasn't, I don't know. I don't care. I'm just glad it's over with.

(He sits back down in his chair, sobbing)

ERNIE It's all right, Ken. We know. Lenny told us.

KEN *(Looking at ERNIE)* You know?

ERNIE Yes.

KEN Who told you?

ERNIE Lenny told us.

KEN Glenn told you?

ERNIE No. Lenny. LENNY. LENNY TOLD US.

CLAIRE I wish he were deaf again.

KEN *(Looks at* LENNY*)* It it true, Lenny? Did you tell them?

LENNY Oh, finish your goddamn dinner and leave us alone, will you?

ERNIE All right, take it easy, Lenny. He's been under a big strain.

LENNY And I haven't? I was acting my goddamn head off that Myra was here. I had actual conversations with her up there. I even did her voice in case someone was listening.

COOKIE Was that you? You could have fooled me.

LENNY I *did.*

COOKIE That's right. You did.

GLENN So you really weren't watching Hitler on PBS?

LENNY No, we stopped everything to watch *The Rise and Fall of Adolf Hitler* . . . I don't believe you people.

GLENN It sounded so real, I believed it.

ERNIE *(To* CASSIE*)* What about you, Mrs. Cooper? *(To* GLENN*)* What's her name?

GLENN Cassie.

ERNIE *(To* CASSIE*)* What about you, Cassie? Did you think something strange was going on?

CASSIE Yes. For about six months now.

ERNIE   What do you mean? *(To* GLENN*)* What does she mean?

GLENN   You have to forgive her. She's still very upset about losing her crystal.

COOKIE   We could call a plumber. They get everything out. Wedding rings, car keys. I had an aunt who lost her dentures down the toilet and they got them out.

CLAIRE   And she wore them?

COOKIE   Well, obviously you clean them.

CLAIRE   They could be blessed by the pope, I wouldn't put them in my mouth again.

GLENN   Unless you're into crystals, you wouldn't understand. Apparently, they have very special properties. You have to wash them in clear spring water. They must be kept in direct sunlight. Cassie scrubs them every night with a soft, wet toothbrush. You never dry them in a towel. You pat them in a sort of leathery cloth. They really are very delicate.

CLAIRE   Have you got them enrolled in a good school yet?

ERNIE   Oh, come on, Claire. If crystals work for her, if they give her a sense of comfort and pleasure, what's wrong with it?

CASSIE   You don't have to defend me, Ernie. Crystals will be here millions of years after this planet is gone.

LENNY If the planet is gone, don't the crystals go with it?

ERNIE Lenny, don't.

CHRIS *(To* GLENN*)* I don't know if this would help her any, but there's a big crystal chandelier in the dining room. Should I mention it to her?

GLENN Thanks, Chris, but I don't think so. Best leave her alone now.

CASSIE *(Coming downstairs)* I'm not dead, you know. I can hear. Maybe Ken can't, but I can.

(She exits into the powder room)

COOKIE I can unscrew the toilet myself. I've done it before.

ERNIE I don't think it's the time or the place to fix toilets, sugar.

CLAIRE Yes. Perhaps another time, another place.

LENNY *(To* COOKIE*)* Bleeding arm and all, Cookie, that was one hell of a meal. My hat's off to you.

GLENN Hear! Hear!

ERNIE *Bravissima!*

CHRIS *Arregeno! Arregeno!*

EVERYONE   I liked the duck. The duck was great. Really crispy. And the pasta was especially good. Didn't you think so? How long did you boil it?

KEN *(He gets up with that mad look on his face again)* Doesn't anybody . . . doesn't *any*body—?

ERNIE   Quiet, everybody. Quiet . . . What is it, Ken? Doesn't anybody what?

KEN   Doesn't anybody—want to go upstairs and see if Charley is still alive? It's been awfully quiet up there, hasn't it?

CLAIRE   How would you know?

KEN   What?

ERNIE   You're right. My God, he's right. We've all been so busy eating and explaining to each other, we forgot all about Charley.

KEN *(Pointing to* ERNIE*)*   YES. *YES.* That's what I'm saying.

LENNY   All right, I'll go up and settle this now.

GLENN   Wait, wait. We're all in a precarious situation. Not only Charley, but a lot of people's futures depend on how we deal with this issue.

CLAIRE   Meaning you?

GLENN   Well, no. Cassie and I were the last ones to arrive. We just heard about it. We're hardly involved.

COOKIE   And Ernie and I were cooking the whole time. Nobody told us. Sorry.

LENNY   I *wanted* to call the police. Ken wouldn't let me call the police. Claire, didn't I want to call the police?

CLAIRE   Lenny wanted to call the police.

CHRIS   So what are you saying? That it's Ken's responsibility? He takes the rap for this?

ALL THE OTHERS   Oh, no. No, of course not . . . We didn't say that . . . Nobody's saying that. I didn't hear anyone say that. No one's accusing anyone of anything.

LENNY   . . . What we're saying is, if it comes down to it, he's the most logical, that's all.

CHRIS   I can't believe this. Ken almost went deaf trying to protect Charley and everyone else here. I expected a little bit more from his friends. My God, what a bunch of wimps . . . Have you heard any of this, Ken?

KEN   Well, answer her, Glenn. Have you?

COOKIE *(She screams, as she bends way over)*   Oh, God! Oh, no! Oh, Christ! Oh, Momma!

LENNY   What is it?

COOKIE   I lost my earrings. My good earrings! My grandmother's earrings!

CHRIS *(Bending over, looking)*   Where did you lose them?

COOKIE   Right here. Right around here.

ERNIE   We'll find them, honey.

CLAIRE   What did they look like?

COOKIE   Old! Very old! With pearls. And a little ruby. *(Starting to cry)* My grandmother gave them to me. I'm sick about this. *(They all get on the floor and crawl around looking for the earrings.* COOKIE *screams)* AHHHH! Oh, God! Oh, my God!

CLAIRE   What?

COOKIE   They're in my hand. *(She shows them)*   I forgot I had them. I'm so stupid. Forgive me, everybody, I'm sorry . . . So, what were we saying?

> *(They all glare at* COOKIE *as they struggle to their feet)*

ERNIE   Glenn, I'm a little worried about your wife. Do you think she's all right?

GLENN   Oh, she's fine. She's just in there trying to figure some way to get back at me. She'll come up with something. *(The powder room door suddenly opens and* CASSIE *stands there with one arm extended up the door. Her hair is brushed over one eye. She looks sexy as hell, with a malevolent grin on her face. Everyone turns to look at her)* Yeah, she's got one.

> *(*CASSIE *goes over to the sofa and sits on the arm next to* LENNY, *practically leaning on him)*

CASSIE Please forgive me, everyone. I know I behaved badly tonight. *(She smiles right at* LENNY. *He smiles back, then looks away)* No, I really did . . . and I apologize. I've had—well, I've had a rough day today, and I'm just not here tonight.

LENNY That's okay. Neither are Charley and Myra.

CASSIE *(She smiles at* LENNY*)* That's funny. That's truly funny, Lenny. I can never think of anything funny. How do you do that?

LENNY *(He's a bit flustered)* I don't know . . . I just . . . *(He sees* CLAIRE *glaring at him)* Can I get up and get you a glass of wine?

CASSIE Why? Do I look like I need one?

CLAIRE Who is she getting back at, Glenn, you or me?

GLENN *(Without looking at* CLAIRE*)* All right, Cassie, cut it out.

CASSIE What do you mean, sweetheart?

GLENN You know what I mean. Push your hair back up and sit on a chair.

CASSIE *(She smiles at* GLENN, *then turns to* LENNY*)* Do you know what he's talking about, Len?

CLAIRE Excuse me. I'm going up to get Charley's gun.

ERNIE Cassie, everyone here is your friend. Why don't you and I go out on the terrace and have a nice quiet talk?

COOKIE *(To* ERNIE*)*   You do and you'll have a back worse than mine.

CASSIE   Oh, my goodness, I see what you're thinking. That is really incredible. Because the exact same thing happened to Glenn and me last week at a cocktail party for the Democratic Fund-raising Committee. There was the nicest woman there—very attractive, very sweet, very refined—and because sometimes I can feel so silly and so insecure, I thought she was coming on to Glenn. They got up to dance and they were as close as freshly laid wallpaper.

GLENN   Okay, Cassie, I think we're going.

(The intercom on the phone buzzes)

KEN *(Holding his chest)*   Excuse me. I must have eaten too quickly.

CHRIS   That was the intercom, Ken. Not you.

LENNY *(Going to the phone)*   I'll get it. *(Picking up the phone)* Hello? . . . Charley? Are you all right? *(To the others)* It's Charley.

KEN   Molly? Who's Molly?

GLENN *(Losing it)*   CHARLEY! CHARLEY! NOT MOLLY!

LENNY *(Into the phone)*   Yes, Charley, we're all here . . . Len, Glenn, Ken, Ernie, Claire, Chris, Cassie, and Cookie.

CLAIRE   Isn't it odd that all the women's names begin with a C?

CHRIS   That's right.

COOKIE   Except Myra.

CHRIS   Her middle name is Clara.

CLAIRE   And the men's names are all the same. Len, Glenn, Ken.

CHRIS   That's right.

CLAIRE   Except for Ernie and Charley.

COOKIE   Charley begins with a C.

ERNIE   What is this, anagrams, for Pete sakes? Let him talk on the phone.

LENNY   Yes, Charlie, I understand. No, it's perfectly reasonable. You do what you have to do . . . We'll be here. *(Hangs up the phone)* He needs more time to think.

KEN   More time to drink? He shouldn't drink with Valium.

GLENN   *(Shouting into* KEN's *ear)*   THINK! THINK! NOT DRINK!

KEN   Oh! Oh, my God! Oh, Jesus!

CHRIS   What? What is it?

KEN   My ears popped! They just opened up. My God, it sounds like the subway in here.

ERNIE   This is remarkable, but I'm having the first headache I've ever had in my life.

COOKIE   I just remembered.

CLAIRE   What?

COOKIE   Ernie's last name is Cusack. It begins with a C.

CLAIRE   You just remembered your husband's last name?

KEN   I can hear my own pulse. It's slightly up, but not too bad.

CASSIE *(She smiles sexily at* KEN*)*   Can I take it, Ken? I'm very good at things like that.

GLENN   I'm warning you, Cassie. You're going to end up in the same place where your crystal is.

CASSIE   Don't threaten me, sweetheart, because I'll start naming names.

GLENN   That's it! That's it! I've got to stay, but I'm putting you in a taxi.

CASSIE *(Screaming)*   Never mind! I'LL WALK!!

> (KEN *grabs his ears in pain and drops to the floor.* CASSIE *storms out the front door)*

95

GLENN   Walk? Twenty-two miles? Cassie, wait for me. Will you wait!!

(He runs out after CASSIE*)*

CLAIRE   I feel badly for her. Especially because one day she'll grow old and die.

COOKIE   I just thought of something else. Glenn went to Penn.

CHRIS   Oh, sit on it, will you, honey?

ERNIE   If I had you all in my group, I would never need another group again.

KEN   *(At the stage right wall, near the window)*   Shh. Quiet. I can hear them.

LENNY   Hear who?

KEN   Glenn and Cassie. They're in the driveway. I swear, I can hear them talking.

CLAIRE   The man is a German shepherd.

ERNIE   I don't think it's your business to listen, Ken.

LENNY   If he can hear through walls, it's his business.

KEN   She's talking about a woman. She's very upset.

COOKIE *(Looking out the window)*   I'll say. She just kicked a car with her foot. Who owns the BMW?

LENNY   Ah, shit. The good side too, I bet.

CHRIS *(Leaping to her feet)* I just figured it out.

CLAIRE I know what she's going to say. Glenn, Ken, and Len are all men.

CHRIS No, no, no. It's Glenn Cooper . . . Glenn is the one that Myra's having the affair with.

COOKIE You think so?

CHRIS Figure it out. Myra's been working very hard on Glenn's campaign. Two, three nights a week. *Late* nights.

CLAIRE Of course. Charley's not dumb. He puts two and two together, confronts Myra with it, she confesses, Charley kicks her out of the house, tells the servants to go home, and tries to blow his brains out.

ERNIE You don't know that. That's an assumption on your part. That is a very, very dangerous statement to make. Don't you agree with me, Len?

LENNY No.

ERNIE Why not?

LENNY I don't feel like it.

ERNIE Listen, I think we have to bring this thing to a head. I'm going to go up and speak to Charley and find out what's what.

(He starts for the stairs)

KEN   Wait a minute. Hold it! As far as Charley's concerned, only Chris and I know about Charley shooting himself in the ear, am I right?

LENNY   Right. He never said a word to me. He had the pillow covering up his ear the whole time.

CLAIRE   So what you're saying is, he doesn't know we know anything.

ERNIE   Well, he's got to know that we all haven't seen Myra. And that there's no servants here.

KEN   Exactly. But he doesn't know the *rest* of you know about the gunshot.

CHRIS   Slower. Go slower. Talk like we're children.

KEN   My point is, I told him we wouldn't tell anybody.

CLAIRE   And then you went ahead and told everybody.

KEN   No, no. I told only you and Lenny. Lenny told everybody.

LENNY   But you were deaf then. You didn't hear me telling everybody.

CLAIRE   *(To* KEN*)*   And then you told everybody *after* Lenny told everybody.

CHRIS   Go fast again. It doesn't make any difference.

(COOKIE *stands up and goes to the window*)

KEN What I'm trying to say is, as long as Charley doesn't think the rest of you know—

ERNIE —why tell him now? I see your point. We've got to keep up the subterfuge. If we confront him with everyone knowing about the gunshot, he could go to pieces. So until he tells us his own story himself, we have to pretend we don't know anything.

KEN I should be the one who goes up. I tell Charley that everyone is here. And he asks me does everyone here know what's happened.

ERNIE You say no.

KEN I say no. Then Charley asks me, "Well, if I'm not down there and Myra's not down there and the help's not down there, what did you tell them?"

COOKIE (*Looking out the window*) Something's wrong with Cassie. Woops.

LENNY Woops? What's woops? She threw up in the car?

COOKIE She hit Glenn. His nose is bleeding.

CLAIRE Tell me when he hits her back. I'd love to watch that.

KEN Will you all please be quiet. I can't hear myself think. What was I saying?

CHRIS (*Quickly*) You said, "I should be the one who goes up. I tell Charley that everyone is here. And he asks, 'Does everyone here know what's happened?' "

Ernie said, "You say no." You said, "I say no. Then Charley asks me, 'Well, if I'm not down there and Myra's not down there—' "

KEN   Alrightalrightalright!!

ERNIE   I've got it. I've got it. Here's what we do. Charley's going to want to know what Ken told us. Ken tells Charley that he told us that Charley had a large benign wart removed from his ear this morning, but he's okay. Then suddenly Myra's mother broke her hip this afternoon and that Myra took her to the hospital and is going to stay there the night. The help, thinking the party was off, left the food and went home. It all happened so fast, they forgot to call us. We all got here, we understood, and decided to cook the dinner ourselves . . . That's the story.

CLAIRE   I wouldn't believe the mother breaking her hip.

ERNIE   Why not?

CLAIRE   She died six years ago.

ERNIE   Then her father broke his hip.

CLAIRE   Her father lives in California.

ERNIE   Does she have a relative in the city?

CHRIS   She has a cousin Florence.

ERNIE   Then Florence broke her hip.

CHRIS   Florence is married. Why didn't her husband take her?

ERNIE   Then Myra broke her hip. The neighbors took her.

COOKIE   If he only had a wart removed, Charley could have taken her.

CLAIRE   Can't you think of something else?

ERNIE *(He is upset)*   *I did!!* I thought of the mother, the father, the cousin, the wart, and the hip. Nothing satisfies you people.

KEN   There's no logic to it. Nothing in that story is plausible.

ERNIE *(Losing it)*   We don't need plausible. The man is in shock, mental anguish, and emotional despair. Logic doesn't mean shit to him right now. *(He sits down, composes himself)* Excuse my language. *(The phone rings. They all look at it. The phone rings again. They all look at each other)* The telephone!

LENNY   Don't you think we know it's a telephone? We all have telephones, Ernie. We're all wealthy people here.

   (The phone is still ringing)

ERNIE   Just calm down, everybody. *(He picks up the phone)* Hello? . . . Yes? . . . Yes, he is . . . Who's calling, please? . . . I see. All right . . . Just a moment, please. *(Covering the phone)* It's a woman. For Glenn.

CLAIRE   So?

ERNIE   It sounds like Myra.

COOKIE   Oh, fuck-a-doodle-doo.

KEN   Should I go get him?

ERNIE   Wait a minute. *(Into the phone)* Er, Glenn is outside just now. Can I tell him who's calling? . . . I see. All right. Hold on. *(Covering the phone)* I can't tell. Maybe it is, maybe it isn't.

COOKIE   What did she say when you asked who's calling?

ERNIE   She said, "Just a friend."

LENNY   How did she say it?

ERNIE   She said, "Just a friend." How many ways are there to say it?

LENNY   I'll tell you how many ways. Nervous, phony, sincere, drunk—

CHRIS   Scared, guilty, lying—

COOKIE   Offhanded, perplexed, deceitful—

CLAIRE   Ominous, anonymous—

ERNIE   THIS ISN'T SCRABBLE, for God's sakes.

LENNY   Let me talk to her.

ERNIE   She didn't ask for you.

LENNY   She didn't ask for you, either. I know Myra's voice. Give me the phone. *(He grabs the phone from*

ERNIE) Hello? . . . No, it isn't. It's Glenn's friend Len
. . . No, Ken is getting Glenn . . . You sound awfully
familiar. Do I know you? . . . I see . . . Well, hold on,
please. *(Covering the phone)* I don't think it's her.

COOKIE   Well, who does it sound like?

LENNY   Meryl Streep.

COOKIE   Meryl Streep? Why would Meryl Streep call
here?

LENNY   I didn't say it *was* Meryl Streep. But you know
how she sounds in the movies? Like she always does the
character perfectly but it's not really her. That's how
she sounds.

COOKIE   Like she's not Meryl Streep?

ERNIE   Now we're playing Trivial Pursuit! This is not
a game show. Ken, will you please get Glenn. *(Grab-
bing the phone back from* LENNY*)* Hello? . . . Somebody
went to get Glenn . . . Hello? . . . *(He hangs up)* She
hung up. She must have gotten suspicious.

KEN   Quiet down everyone. I hear something!

CLAIRE   I'll bet it's the Concorde landing in London.

KEN   It's a car coming up the driveway.

   (We see headlights flash on the window)

CLAIRE   Maybe it's Myra.

LENNY   Maybe it's Harry and Joan from Venezuela.

> *(The front door opens quickly and* GLENN *rushes in, holding a bloody hankie to his nose)*

GLENN   We got trouble. Oh, God, have we got trouble.

KEN   What is it?

GLENN   The police. It's a police car.

LENNY *(Loudly, pointing at* KEN*)*   Okay! I warned you! I *told* you we should have called the police. Now look what's happened. The police came.

KEN   Who could have called the police?

CLAIRE   Maybe it was Myra.

CHRIS   Maybe it was Charley.

LENNY   Maybe it was Cassie. *(To* GLENN*)* You were fighting with her, weren't you? Did she use the phone in my car?

GLENN   Not to call. She hit me with it.

LENNY   She broke my phone? My new phone in my new car?

ERNIE   Will everybody calm down? We've got to figure out what to say when they come in.

COOKIE *(Looking out the window)*   They're trying to talk to Cassie. She won't roll down the windows.

LENNY *My* windows? They're going to bust my windows? I'm going to take my car home in an envelope.

ERNIE *(To* GLENN*)* Why did you leave her out there in the car? She's in no condition to answer police questions.

GLENN She's in good enough condition to smash my nose . . . Goddamn, I got blood on my shirt.

LENNY And you're running for the state senate? I wouldn't let you run for Chinese food.

CHRIS What's wrong with you people? I've got a six-year-old child at home who behaves better than we do.

LENNY Fine! Then get him over here and tell *him* to talk to the police.

KEN Take it easy, Len. She's been doing her share. She's the one who called Dr. Dudley.

LENNY EVERYBODY CALLED DR. DUDLEY. HE'S IN THE YELLOW PAGES IN CHINA!!

CLAIRE Maybe Dudley called the police.

(The telephone rings)

ERNIE It's the phone again.

LENNY He's right. He guessed it was the phone twice in a row. This genius is going to save our lives.

ERNIE *(Picking up the phone)*   Hello? . . . Yes? . . . Just a minute, please. *(To* GLENN*)* Glenn, it's for you. *(Announcing to the group)* It's the same woman who called before.

GLENN *(Going to the phone)*   What same woman?

CLAIRE   She wouldn't say. Maybe it was Myra, maybe it was Meryl Streep.

GLENN   Meryl Streep?

CLAIRE   You know how she sounds in the movies? Like she always does the character perfectly, but it's not really her? That's how this person sounded.

LENNY *(At the front door, looking out)*   We've got two policemen coming in, she's giving us a résumé of the party.

COOKIE *(Looking out the window)*   Oh, oh. They're walking over here.

GLENN *(Into the phone)*   Hello?

COOKIE *(Hobbling away from the window)*   They're on the way over.

GLENN *(Into the phone)*   Oh, hi. How are you? . . . No, it's not a cold, it's a telephone injury.

KEN   Now listen. The thing we can't do is let them see Charley. We can't let him downstairs or them upstairs.

GLENN *(Into the phone)*   I tried talking to Cassie, but she's very upset.

ERNIE *(Gesturing importantly)* Above all, no false state-
ments. We must keep within the law. This above all,
agreed?

LENNY *(Mocking* ERNIE's *gestures)* Yea! To thine own
self be true. Wherein the hearts of better men—are you
fucking crazy? They're outside the door.

GLENN *(Into the phone)* Of course I think you should talk
to her, but I can't get her out of the car.

KEN They're going to ask about the gunshots. What do
we tell them about the gunshots?

GLENN *(Into the phone)* All right, I'll call you back in
fifteen minutes. Are you at the 914 number?

LENNY Kill him! Somebody kill him! Choke him with
the telephone wire.

(The doorbell chimes)

CHRIS I'm very serious about this, but I'm not going to
be able to hold my bladder.

ERNIE All right, I've got it. We tell them we never heard
the gunshots.

CLAIRE You mean lie to them?

LENNY What happened to "this above all"?

ERNIE It won't work tonight. Maybe some other time.

CHRIS If you let me go to the bathroom, I promise I'll
come back.

GLENN *(He's still on the phone)* Listen, I know you're a good friend. And I thank you for all your wonderful support.

LENNY Leave him here. Let's run for our lives and leave that schmuck for the cops.

GLENN *(Into the phone)* I can't talk anymore. I'll call you back later . . . I will . . . Good-bye. *(He hangs up and turns to the others)* All right, what's going on?

LENNY Well, about six weeks ago we got an invitation to this party—

ERNIE Stop it, Lenny . . . All right, think everybody. Think. Why didn't we hear the gunshots?

COOKIE *(Raising her hand)* We're all deaf people. We meet once a week. That's why we didn't hear the doorbell.

LENNY *(To CLAIRE)* Now you know why they call her Cookie.

CHRIS I've got it! We were listening to the Hitler program. The cannons were bombing Berlin, we couldn't hear anything else.

(They all consider this)

LENNY THERE WAS NO HITLER PROGRAM. WE MADE THE FUCKING THING UP TO FOOL THIS ASSHOLE.

(He points to GLENN)

GLENN Hey, I've had just about enough from you, Lenny.

(The doorbell chimes. They all drop to the floor)

KEN We've got to let them in.

LENNY All right. Claire, open the door.

CLAIRE I can't. I'm in charge of the music.

GLENN The music! That's it!

CHRIS What is?

GLENN The music was on. We were all dancing. We couldn't hear the gunshots. Claire, put on the music.

(CLAIRE goes to the stereo cabinet)

KEN *(To CLAIRE)* WAIT!! Don't turn it on yet. There's one last thing to do.

CLAIRE What?

KEN Somebody has to be Charley. Just in case.

LENNY Just in case what?

KEN Just in case the police want to speak to Charley.

ERNIE Ken is right. Charley is in no condition to tell them the real story.

LENNY Of course not, because no one has *heard* the real story yet.

KEN   Exactly. But we have to be sure whatever story the police hear has to be one that's not going to get us all in trouble.

CHRIS   I never saw a sinking ship empty so fast.

GLENN   I agree. Ken is absolutely right. *(To the men)* One of you three guys has to be Charley.

LENNY   When did *you* move to France?

GLENN   Well, let's be honest. I never even heard the gunshots.

LENNY   *(Shouting in* GLENN's *ear)*   BANG BANG, you bastard!

COOKIE   Isn't it against the law to impersonate another real person?

ERNIE   Yes it is, dear, but not if you do it well.

CHRIS   *(To the women)*   Can you believe we actually married these men?

LENNY   This is a major felony we're talking about. You want to spend thirty years in a maximum-security prison wearing a tuxedo?

KEN   *(Coming downstage and taking charge)*   We're all in this together, Glenn. Here's how we do it. You put out two fingers or one finger. If three guys are the same and one is different, that guy is Charley . . . Are we ready?

LENNY   Who made you Don Corleone?

KEN   You have a better idea?

LENNY   Yeah. Let the women wrestle for it.

GLENN   Come on. Let's get it over with, for crisssakes.

KEN   Okay. Here we go. One—two—three! *(The men put out fingers)* Two and two. No good . . . Try again. Ready? One—two—three! *(The men put out fingers)* All the same. No good . . . Again! *(The doorbell rings)* Ready? One—two—three! *(The men put out fingers)* Aha! Lenny!

LENNY *(Quickly putting his hand behind his back)*   What do you mean Lenny?

GLENN   We all have two fingers out, you have one finger.

LENNY   Bullshit! I had two stuck together. *(He shows them)*   I got duck grease on my fingers.

ERNIE   It was one finger, Lenny.

LENNY   It was two, I swear to God.

ERNIE   No, no. It was one. ONE FINGER. ONE! I SAW IT!!

COOKIE   And that man graduated from Johns Hopkins.

GLENN   Go on upstairs, Lenny. And don't come down unless we call you.

LENNY   *I had a better time in my car accident.*

   (He goes into Charley's *room and closes the door. The doorbell rings again*)

KEN   Okay, Claire, put on the music.

ERNIE   Let's go, kids. Hurry up. Get your partners. *(They do)* Okay.

> *(*CLAIRE *turns on the stereo. It is a loud rendition of "La Bamba." . . . The three couples dance furiously. We hear loud banging on the front door, and then it opens. Two police officers stand there. One,* OFFICER WELCH, *is a strong, vigorous man. The other,* OFFICER PUDNEY, *is a woman in her late twenties. They stand watching the couples dance. No one seems to notice the police)*

WELCH   *(Yelling)*   Can you shut that thing off, please! *(No one notices)* SOMEBODY PLEASE SHUT THAT DAMN THING OFF!

> *(*KEN *turns the music off. They all look surprised that the police are in the room)*

ERNIE *(Indignantly)*   I beg your pardon. May I ask what you're doing here?

WELCH   I'm sorry. I didn't mean to bust the door open.

ERNIE   Then why didn't you ring first?

WELCH   I did. Five times.

ERNIE (Moving near the police)   Five times? We didn't hear it.

WELCH   I guess the music was on so loud, you couldn't hear anything.

ERNIE Of *course*. The *music*.

KEN That's why we didn't hear you.

CLAIRE No wonder we didn't get any phone calls. We couldn't hear them.

CHRIS That's what it was. The music.

COOKIE It was on . . .

EVERYONE . . . *so loud.*

ERNIE *(Congenially)* Now, what seems to be the trouble, Officer?

WELCH Well, just sort of routine investigation, sir. My name is Officer Welch. This is Officer Pudney. Is this your house, sir?

ERNIE *My* house? No, no. I live elsewhere. Other than here.

KEN As do I. Live elsewhere. Could you tell us what this is about, Officer?

EVERYONE Yes, what's this about? Is anything wrong? Why are the police here? I can't imagine what's going on.

WELCH All right, all right, take it easy. Calm down. I just want to ask a few questions . . . May I ask who the owner of this house is?

KEN   We'd be delighted to tell, Officer, but I believe it's customary first for you to inform us as to why these questions are being asked of us.

WELCH   You're a lawyer, aren't you.

KEN   Yes, I am.

WELCH   Well, as a lawyer you understand you're not obligated to answer these questions. I was hoping someone would be cooperative enough to tell me the owner's name.

(*They all look at each other*)

CLAIRE   Brock. Charley Brock.

WELCH   Could you tell me if Mr. Brock is at home at present?

(*They all look at each other*)

CLAIRE   I'm not sure. Chris, is Charley at home?

CHRIS   Charley? I think he went to walk the dog.

WELCH   Then he'll be back soon?

COOKIE   I don't think so. It's a dachshund. They take very small steps.

KEN   (*Wanting no trouble*)   He's home. He came back, Officer.

WELCH   Well, then could I possibly see Mr. Brock for a moment?

KEN *(Coming downstage, taking charge)* Well, it's an awkward time, Officer. As you can see, we're celebrating a party.

WELCH Yes, I've noticed. What's the occasion?

KEN The tenth wedding anniversary of Charley and Myra Brock.

WELCH *(Moving toward* KEN*)* I wouldn't take long. I just need a minute of his time.

KEN Well, unfortunately, Mr. Brock is sleeping.

WELCH Sleeping? In the middle of his anniversary party?

KEN He was feeling depressed. He took a sleeping pill.

WELCH Well, could I see *Mrs.* Brock?

KEN Mrs. Brock is not here.

WELCH She's not?

KEN That's why Mr. Brock is depressed.

WELCH Where is she?

> *(They all look at each other)*

ERNIE . . . Her father broke his hip. She had to take him to the hospital.

> *(They all glare at him)*

WELCH   During her anniversary party? Couldn't someone *else* take him to the hospital?

CLAIRE   Her father lives in California.

CHRIS   It has to do with cousins and warts and hips. It's
very complicated.

WELCH *(Moving toward* GLENN, *who is hiding his face with
his hand)*   You, sir? Something wrong with your eye?

GLENN   Me? Yes. I put some drops in tonight and the cap
fell off. Most of the bottle went in.

WELCH   May I have your name, sir?

GLENN   My name?

WELCH   Yes, sir.

GLENN   You mean, my name?

WELCH   Yes, sir . . . Is there a problem with giving me
your name?

GLENN   I'm sorry. I just can't see you very well.

WELCH   You don't have to see to talk, sir. The drops
didn't go in your mouth, did they?

KEN   Officer, I feel you're being unnecessarily abusive to
these people. If you're going to ask any more questions,
you'll have to tell us what this is all about.

WELCH   Yes, sir. I will . . . Can you please tell me who owns the BMW outside?

CLAIRE   It's my husband's car.

WELCH   And what is his name, please?

KEN   You don't have to answer that, Claire.

CLAIRE   His name is Len. Leonard Ganz.

WELCH   And where is Mr. Ganz now?

KEN *(Like in court)*   I object.

WELCH *(He is annoyed)*   I ain't a judge! This ain't a court! I don't have a gavel! I just want to know where the man is.

KEN   You still haven't told us what this is about, so we're still not telling you where Mr. Ganz is.

WELCH   I don't know why I always have trouble in this neighborhood . . . Okay . . . *(Consulting his notebook)* At approximately eight-fifteen tonight, an auto accident occurred on twelfth and Danbury. A brand-new red 1990 Porsche convertible with New York license plates smashed into the side of a brand-new BMW four-door sedan. Now, we know it wasn't the BMW's fault because the Porsche was a stolen car. Stolen at eight-fifteen tonight right off the dealer's lot. The man and the Porsche got away. Now do you know who that brand-new Porsche belonged to?

CLAIRE   How would I know?

WELCH   It belonged to Deputy Mayor Charles M. Brock. Purchased today as a gift from his wife, Myra. A surprise wedding anniversary present.

CLAIRE   Surprise hardly says it.

KEN   Aha! So, you're here to investigate the car accident?

WELCH   That's right. Now if Mr. Ganz is here, I'd like to speak to him. And if he's not here, the police department would like to know where he is.

KEN   I see . . . Do you think you could wait outside for one moment, Officer?

WELCH   Why?

KEN   Mrs. Ganz is my client. I would like to consult with her before any further questioning. It's within my rights.

WELCH   . . . One minute. That's all you get.

(WELCH *motions to* PUDNEY *and they go out the front door*)

KEN   All right, we don't have much time. One of us has to be Lenny.

ERNIE   What are you talking about?

KEN   The man doesn't even know about the gunshots. He just wants to ask Lenny about the accident. But Lenny can't be Lenny because we need Lenny to be Charley in case he wants to ask Charley about the new car, and we can't let him see Charley because Charley has a bullet hole in his ear.

COOKIE *(To* CHRIS*)*   Chris, do you understand him in real life?

CHRIS   We don't actually talk that much.

KEN   All right. Glenn! Ernie! We have to choose again.

ERNIE   Oh, leave me alone with this stupid game.

   *(*ERNIE *walks away)*

KEN   I know it's stupid, but we have to do it. We need a Lenny.

CHRIS *(To the men)*   Never mind. The girls will do it. Come on, girls. The odd woman's husband is Lenny.

CLAIRE   My husband *is* Lenny.

CHRIS   No, Lenny is Charley. You're playing for Glenn. Get in a circle.

   (The women bunch together, just like the men)

COOKIE   I don't know how to play this.

CHRIS   Just put out your fingers. We'll do the counting . . . Odd finger loses . . . All right? Ready? One—two— three. *(They all put out fingers except* COOKIE, *who puts out a fist)* No! . . . No no no no! Your fingers, Cookie, open your fist.

COOKIE   I don't want to lose my earrings again.

CHRIS   Just one or two fingers! All right? Here we go.
One—two—three! *(They all put out fingers)* Aha! It's
me! Fuck! . . . Sorry, Ken.

KEN   It's okay. All right, I'm Lenny. Open the door,
Ernie.

> *(ERNIE goes to the front door. The door opens. WELCH
> and PUDNEY come in. WELCH is unhappy)*

WELCH   I'm glad to see you're not dancing again. Now
where is Mr. Leonard Ganz?

KEN   He's right here in this room. I am Leonard Ganz.

WELCH *(Looking at him sideways)*   You are?

KEN   Yes.

WELCH   How come it took you a whole minute to think
of your name?

KEN   Never rush your answers. Harvard Law School.

WELCH   Never trust a man who doesn't know if he's here
or not. Police Academy. *(CHRIS involuntarily puts her
arm through KEN's to protect him. WELCH sees this)* Who
are you, ma'am?

CHRIS   I'm his wife. His wife's best friend. *(Pointing to
CLAIRE)* Her. Mrs. Ganz. *(She takes her arm away)*

WELCH   Are you here alone, ma'am?

CHRIS   No. I'm here with my husband, Mr. Gorman.

WELCH   Where is he?

CHRIS *(She looks around)*   He must have gone home early.

WELCH   Not much of a party, is it?

CHRIS   It's had its ups and downs.

WELCH *(To* KEN)   All right, Mr. Ganz. Tell us about the accident. In full and complete detail.

KEN   . . . Do you think you could step outside just one more time?

WELCH   I AIN'T GOING NO PLACE NO WHERE NO TIME!!! THIS IS IT!! This is where I live till I get what I came for, even if my whole family has to move in. *(We hear the walkie-talkie squawk in* PUDNEY'S *holster)* What's that?

PUDNEY   1047 Pudney. Over . . . *(The walkie-talkie squawks)* Check . . . Got it . . . Hold it. *(To* WELCH) Red 1990 Porsche convertible located at Fifth and Market in Tarrytown. Suspect apprehended. They said call it a night.

WELCH *(He nods)*   Well, I guess that ties that little bundle up.

EVERYONE   Isn't that wonderful? Terrific! I'm so happy.

WELCH   Sorry to disturb you, folks.

EVERYONE   Hey, it's okay. No problem. We understand.

WELCH   There'll be some further questioning for you tomorrow, Mr. Ganz. No need to take any more of your time tonight. Thank you and goodnight, folks.

EVERYONE   It's okay. Our pleasure. Anytime, Officer.

(GLENN *goes to* WELCH *and shakes his hand*)

WELCH   I *know* I've seen you some place before. What's your name again?

GLENN *(Happily)*   Glenn. Glenn Cooper.

WELCH   Were you ever on TV?

GLENN   Well, as a matter of fact, yes. I'm running for the state senate.

WELCH   Right. I saw you do an interview on PBS.

WELCH   Why were you so afraid to give me your name?

GLENN   Well, you know. When you're in politics, you don't want to get mixed up with these things.

WELCH   Yes, but you weren't involved with this. Unless you witnessed the accident. Did you?

GLENN   No, no, no. My wife and I arrived late. We didn't even hear the gunshots.

(*There is a moment of frozen silence. The others look to heaven for help*)

WELCH   . . . What gunshots?

GLENN   Hmmm?

WELCH   I said, what gunshots?

GLENN   I suppose the gunshots that were fired when they chased the stolen car?

WELCH   That was twelve miles away over in Tarrytown. You got twenty-twenty hearing, Mr. Cooper?

(PUDNEY's *walkie-talkie squawks again*)

PUDNEY   1047 Pudney. Over . . . *(She listens. The walkie-talkie squawks)* Right . . . Check . . . Will do. *(She turns it off. To* WELCH*)* Neighbors reported two gunshots were fired about nine p.m. *from inside 1257 Peekskill Road, Sneden's Landing. Investigate.*

WELCH   1257 Peekskill Road . . . Well, we've got ourselves a double header, don't we? . . . Anybody want to tell us about the gunshots?

EVERYONE   No. Not really. We didn't hear any gunshots. The music was so loud.

WELCH   Nobody heard them, I suppose. *(To* GLENN*)* Who's the woman sitting outside in the BMW?

GLENN   She's my wife, Cassie.

WELCH   I'd like to have a little talk with Mrs. Cooper . . . Connie, get her in here.

COOKIE *(Portentously)*   Connie? With a C?

(PUDNEY *exits through the front door*)

WELCH *(Coming downstage)* Looks to me like you all had a fine dinner . . . I'd like to speak to the help, please.

KEN There is no help.

WELCH Then who did the cooking?

COOKIE I did.

WELCH What's your name?

COOKIE Cookie.

WELCH I mean your real name.

COOKIE That *is* my real name. I have two sisters named Candy and Taffy. I swear to God.

WELCH *(He looks at* KEN*)* Is that blood on your shirt, Len?

KEN Blood? Oh, yes. I cut myself with a fork during dinner.

WELCH *(He nods doubtingly and looks at* GLENN*)* Is that blood on *your* shirt, Glenn?

GLENN Oh. Yes. I must have rubbed against Len . . . when we were dancing.

WELCH Ken, Len, and Glenn. That's really weird.

KEN It's just a coincidence.

WELCH I guess it is. My name is Ben. *(The front door opens, and* CASSIE *comes in with* PUDNEY. CASSIE *is still angry. The shoulder pad on her suit jacket has been ripped open at the seam, and the white padding hangs out)* Are you all right, Mrs. Cooper?

CASSIE I'm not pressing any charges. My lawyer will handle this.

GLENN It was an accident. She dropped the electric cigarette lighter in the car on the leather seat, and I grabbed her jacket to pull her out of the car.

WELCH *(To* GLENN*)* And how'd you get that nasty blow on your nose?

GLENN My wife was hanging up the car phone in the dark and my head was a little too low.

WELCH My my my. We got a lot of cartoon humor in this case, don't we?

COOKIE *(In pain, as she tries to sit)* Ahhhh!

WELCH You hurtin' too, ma'am?

COOKIE Oh, I have a chronic back spasm. It's very hard for me to sit, stand, or walk.

WELCH And you didn't hear the gunshots either, I suppose?

COOKIE No. I was dancing. *(*WELCH *looks at her in disbelief)* Dancing is good for my back.

125

WELCH   And to think I was almost out the door with this one. *(To* CHRIS*)* Mrs. Gorman?

CHRIS   Is that me? *(She looks around)* Yes. Mrs. Gorman. Right.

WELCH   And what do you do?

CHRIS   Well, mostly, I've been helping with the drinks.

WELCH   Your occupation!

CHRIS   Oh, nothing . . . No, not nothing. I'm a liar—a lawyer! . . . Sorry . . . And I'm a mother. I have two children . . . A boy . . . No, one child . . . Sorry, I'm very nervous.

WELCH   You and everybody else, ma'am. I'm going to say something now that is not really a part of my official capacity. But I don't believe one goddamn thing I've heard in this room. I think there were gunshots here tonight. I think someone or *everyone* is trying to cover up something. A man gets hit in the nose, another man stabs himself with a fork, someone's BMW gets smashed up, the host takes a short-legged dog for a walk and then goes to sleep, the hostess takes her father to a hospital in California with a broken hip, and nobody hears two gunshots because everybody is dancing, including a woman named Cookie who's been cooking all night who can't stand or walk! You people have to deal with me. I'm a real cop, you understand? I'm not somebody named Elmer that your kids watch on the Disney Channel . . . Now, I want some *real* answers, intelligent answers, believable answers, and answers that don't make me laugh. But first, I want to see Mr. Charley Brock and find out what the hell's going on here—including the possibility of him having two bullet holes in him. Now, I'll give you five seconds to get him down here, or I'll take two seconds and go upstairs and find him. *(KEN and GLENN argue silently behind WELCH's back)* Don't mess with me now. I'm so close to a promotion, I can smell it. And I'm not going to screw it up with *this* case . . . Do I start counting or do I start climbing up steps? It's up to you.

(Nobody moves. WELCH starts up the steps)

GLENN   Okay, just wait, will you? Wait a second. Wait. Okay? Can you wait? Just wait . . . Ernie! Ken! I mean Len. I think it's time to call Charley and ask him to come down, don't you?

ERNIE   Definitely.

KEN   Absolutely.

(ERNIE goes to the phone and rings CHARLEY's room)

ERNIE   . . . Charley? . . . It's Ernie . . . We're ready for you now . . . Are you ready for us now? . . . Relax, Charley, that's just an hysteric nerve reaction.

KEN   What's wrong with him?

ERNIE *(To KEN)*   He thinks he went temporarily blind. *(Into the phone)* Just put some cold water on your eyes and come down. There are two police officers who want to speak to you . . . Why? . . . BECAUSE YOU PUT OUT ONE FINGER, THAT'S WHY!! *(Hanging up and smiling at WELCH)* He's fine. He's coming down.

GLENN   The truth is, Officer, we were trying to protect Mr. Brock because he's a dear friend of ours. But we know we're all in jeopardy if we hold back the truth. *(Moving away from* WELCH*)* There *were* two gunshots here tonight. I, personally, did not hear them, but I share equal blame with those who *did* hear the shots and did not come forth with that information . . . despite the fact that I didn't hear them.

KEN   Stop helping us so much, Glenn.

GLENN   Nevertheless, Mr. Brock is willing to tell us the full and complete story, the details of which none of us has heard yet. About the missing help, about the disappearance of his wife, Myra, and about the two gunshots, which I didn't hear.

COOKIE   Oh, God, I'm getting another spasm in my back.

CHRIS   Oh, who gives a shit?

> *(*CHARLEY*'s bedroom door opens.* LENNY *stands there as* CHARLEY, *wearing a robe, pajamas, and slippers, and a large bandage over his ear. They all look at him. He looks at them, furious for making him do this)*

GLENN   Hello, Charley.

KEN   Hi, Charley.

ERNIE   Feeling all right, Charley?

> *(*LENNY *comes slowly down the stairs)*

WELCH I'm Officer Welch, Mr. Brock. This is Officer Pudney. Please sit down. *(LENNY sits)* Take this down, Connie. *(She takes out her notebook)* Now, Mr. Brock, tell us from the beginning exactly what happened in this house tonight.

COOKIE Does anyone want coffee and lemon tarts?

LENNY Yes, a tart would be wonderful.

WELCH Not now, ma'am . . . Go ahead, Mr. Brock.

LENNY Okay . . . Let's see . . . the story . . . as it happened . . . as I remember it . . . as I'm telling it . . . Well, here goes . . . At exactly six o'clock tonight I came home from work. My wife, Myra, was in her dressing room getting dressed for the party. I got a bottle of champagne from the refrigerator and headed upstairs. Rosita, our Spanish cook, was in the kitchen with Ramona, her Spanish sister, and Romero, her Spanish son. They were preparing an Italian dinner. They were waiting for Myra to tell them when to start the dinner. As I climbed the stairs, I said to myself, "It's my tenth wedding anniversary and I can't believe I still love my wife so much." Myra was putting on the perfume I bought her for Christmas. I purposely buy it because it drives me crazy . . . I tapped on her door. Tap tap tap. She opens it. I hand her a glass of champagne. I make a toast. *(Looking at CLAIRE)* "To the most beautiful wife a man ever had for ten years." She says, "To the best man and the best ten years a beautiful wife ever had." . . . We drink. We kiss. We toast again. "To the loveliest skin on the loveliest body that has never aged a day in ten wonderful years." . . . She toasts, "To the gentlest hands that ever stroked the loveliest skin that never has aged in ten wonderful years." . . . We drink. We kiss. We toast . . . We drink. We kiss. We toast . . . By seven o'clock the bottle is finished, my wife is sloshed, and I'm completely toasted . . . And then I smell the perfume. The perfume I could never resist . . . I loved her in that moment with as much passion and ardor as the night we were first newlyweds. *(He rises. To* WELCH) I tell you this, not with embarrassment, but with pride and joy for a love that grows stronger and more lasting as each new day passes. We lay there spent, naked in each other's arms, complete in our happiness. It's now eight o'clock and outside it's grown dark. Suddenly, a gentle knock on the door. Knock knock knock. The door opens and a strange young man looks down at us, with a knife in his hands. Myra screams. *(He begins to act out the story)* I jump up and run for the gun in my drawer. Myra grabs a towel and shields herself. I rush back in with the pistol, ready to save my wife's life. The strange young man says in Spanish, *"Yo quito se dablo enchilada por quesa in quinto minuto."* But I don't speak Spanish and I never saw Rosita's son, Romero, before, and I didn't know the knife was to cut up the salad and he was asking should they heat up the dinner now? So I aimed my gun at him, Myra screams and pulls my arm. The gun goes off and shoots me in the earlobe. Rosita's son, Romero, runs downstairs and tells Rosita and Ramona, *"Mamaseeta! Meela que paso el hombre ay baco ay yah. El hombre que loco, que bang-bang"*—the crazy man took a shot at him. So, Rosita, Ramona, and Romero leave in a huff. My earlobe is bleeding all over Myra's new dress. Suddenly we hear a car pull up. It's the first guests. Myra grabs a bathrobe and runs downstairs to stop Rosita,

Ramona, and Romero, otherwise we'll have no dinner. But they drive off in their Alfa Romeo. I look out
the window, but it's dark and I think someone is
stealing my beautiful old Mercedes, so I take another
shot at them. Myra runs down to the basement where
we keep the cedar chest. She's looking for the dress
she wore last year for Bonds for Israel. She can't find
the light, trips down the stairs, and passes out in the
dark. I run downstairs looking for Myra, notice the
basement door is open, and am afraid the strange-
looking kid is coming back, so I lock the door, not
knowing that Myra is still down there. Then I run
upstairs to take some aspirin because my earlobe is
killing me from the hole in it. But the blood on my
fingers gets in my eyes and by mistake I take four
Valium instead. I hear the guests downstairs and I
want to tell them to look for Myra. But suddenly, I
can't talk from the Valium, and I'm bleeding on the
white rug. So I start to write a note explaining what
happened, but the note looks like gibberish. And I'm
afraid they'll think it was a suicide note and they'll
call the police and my friend Glenn Cooper was coming and it would be very bad for his campaign to get
mixed up with a suicide, so I tore up the note and
flushed it down the toilet, just as they walked into my
room. They're yelling at me, "What happened? What
happened?" And before I could tell them what happened, I passed out on the bed. And that's the whole
goddamn story, as sure as my name is . . . *(He opens
his robe to expose the monogram "CB" on the pajamas)*
. . . Charley Brock.

WELCH *(Moving toward* LENNY*)* I buy it. I buy the
whole thing. You know why I buy it? I buy it because
I *liked* it! I didn't *believe* it, but I liked it! I love my wife,

too, and that's why I want to get home early . . . *(Going to the front door)* . . . Sorry to bother you, folks. Take care of that ear, Mr. Brock, and happy anniversary.

> (WELCH *and* PUDNEY *leave. The others turn and look at* LENNY)

GLENN Where—where in the whole wide world did you find the guts to tell a story like that?

LENNY *(Beaming)* I made it up.

KEN Of *course* you made it up. But when?

LENNY As I was telling it. Sentence by sentence. Word by word. I didn't know where the hell I was going, but I just kept going.

> *(We hear the police car drive away)*

CLAIRE You don't even speak Spanish.

LENNY I made the Spanish up, too.

CHRIS You shit, we all could have gone to jail for perjury.

LENNY *(Smiling)* I know. That was the challenge. The ultimate chutzpah. It was the best goddamn time I ever had in my life.

ERNIE I am impressed. I am sincerely and deeply impressed. You have, without a doubt, Lenny, one of the weirdest minds I've ever come across.

CLAIRE *(Holding up her glass)* A toast to my husband, Lenny. Just when I was getting bored with our marriage, I fell in love with him all over again.

EVERYONE To Lenny!

CHRIS I have an interesting question.

COOKIE What?

CHRIS What do you think really happened to Charley and Myra?

(The intercom buzzes)

ERNIE *(He picks it up)* Hello? . . . Yes, Charley . . . We're all here . . . Are you up to having some visitors? . . . Wonderful . . . We're dying to hear the story. We're on the way. *(He hangs up)* Charley is going to tell us the entire story.

(They all begin to troupe upstairs)

CHRIS I hope it's shorter than Lenny's story.

CASSIE *(To GLENN)* Can we go back later and look for my crystal, honey?

GLENN *(As they go upstairs)* I'll buy you a thousand crystals, angel.

(As they go up the stairs, suddenly we hear a knock from inside the basement door. They all stop and turn)

133

MYRA *(From behind the door)*   Open the door! Open the door! Let me out!

KEN   Who is it?

MYRA *(From behind the door)*   It's Myra!

(They all look at LENNY *in disbelief)*
Curtain

Since 1960, a Broadway season without a Neil Simon comedy or musical has been a rare one. His first play was *Come Blow Your Horn*, followed by the musical *Little Me*. During the 1966–67 season, *Barefoot in the Park*, *The Odd Couple*, *Sweet Charity*, and *The Star-Spangled Girl* were all running simultaneously; in the 1970–71 season, Broadway theatergoers had their choice of *Plaza Suite*, *Last of the Red Hot Lovers*, and *Promises, Promises*. Next came *The Gingerbread Lady*, *The Prisoner of Second Avenue*, *The Sunshine Boys*, *The Good Doctor*, *God's Favorite*, *California Suite*, *Chapter Two*, *They're Playing Our Song*, *I Ought to Be in Pictures*, *Fools*, a revival of *Little Me*, *Brighton Beach Memoirs*, *Biloxi Blues* (which won the Tony Award for Best Play), the female version of *The Odd Couple*, *Broadway Bound*, and *Rumors*.

NEIL SIMON began his writing career in television, writing for *The Phil Silvers Show* and Sid Caesar's *Your Show of Shows*. Mr. Simon has also written for the screen: the adaptations of *Barefoot in the Park*, *The Odd Couple*, *Plaza Suite*, *Last of the Red Hot Lovers*, *The Prisoner of Second Avenue*, *The Sunshine Boys*, *California Suite*, *Chapter Two*, *I Ought to Be in Pictures*, *Brighton Beach Memoirs*, and *Biloxi Blues*. His other screenplays include *After the Fox*, *The Out-of-Towners*, *The Heartbreak Kid*, *Murder by Death*, *The Goodbye Girl*, *The Cheap Detective*, *Seems Like Old Times*, *Only When I Laugh*, and *Max Dugan Returns*.

The author lives in California and New York. He is married to Diane Lander and has three daughters, Ellen, Nancy, and Bryn.